Disability

Theatre
from the InsideOut

Michael &

Erica

Ruth Bieber

with contribution from author Leslie Fanelli

Ruth

chipmunkapublishing
the mental health publisher

Published by
Chipmunkapublishing

http://www.chipmunkapublishing.com

Copyright © Ruth Bieber 2013

Edited by Nick Rainsford

ISBN 978-1-84991-947-0

Chipmunkapublishing gratefully acknowledge the support of Arts Council England.

Table of Contents

Ruth Bieber

Acknowledgements

First and foremost, I am grateful to all my eclectic readers, as a result of a Canadian author, an American contributor and a publisher from the United Kingdom. This trio, has no doubt made for 'creative' reading, both in content and style. As 'social change artists' we are united; I am indebted to each and every one of you.

To Leslie Fanelli, my soul sister in theatre and in life, who exquisitely breathed the final vitality into this "mighty book," as she called it, with her insights and tireless editorial support; many thanks.

To Nicky Peeters, Christopher Sveistrup (G.N.), and Leah Bowen, together with Bonnie Osoff-Bultz (Board Chair), for believing enough in the importance of the work to have it continue after my departure in 2009: without this passionate and fun-loving team, I wouldn't have been able to move on from my creation.

To Dr. Roy Brown for his on-going support and belief in the work of InsideOut Theatre, for his tireless research in the area of quality of life for all, also for contributing the foreword to this book; I am eternally grateful.

To Dr. Bernie Warren, who planted the seeds of inspiration with his firm belief in the right to creative expression for all people; this insight altered my life forever.

To all the actors, students, support practitioners, facilitators, Board Members, and agencies who supported and participated in the InsideOut Theatre programs; your forethought and courage made it all possible.

To Dr. Roberta Jackson, English Department, University of Calgary, for her initial editorial support, her input got me stepping in the right direction, especially with respect to the theme of Feminism.

To Carol Curties, Drama Instructor, Mount Royal University, for her brilliant insights, which make the book accessible to a broader readership; thank you.

To Susan Farmer, for the skillful transcribing of the scripts and for her love of Theatre and Shamanism; many thanks.

To artist, Maggie Shirley, for creatively and skillfully designing the cover of the book; thank you.

At long last, to the chorus of Angels, who sung the ultimate clarity into this book after my eleventh hour decision to totally restructure the entire manuscript. I am indebted to Wolfione, Ann Denglis, Lisa Hilbrecht and Janet Fidler. Also to 'Mary Oxendale Spensley' who brought along Coyote to shake up ideas that were considered finished. Long live the Trickster!

To the Canadian National Institute for the Blind, for presenting me with the Euclid Harry Leadership Award, which bought me some time to complete this book.

To the Calgary Foundation, for the generous support which helped fund the many typists, transcribers, and editorial supports over the years. To the Alberta Arts Career Scholarship Fund which provided much needed support in completing the final draft.

Finally, many thanks to Chipmunka Publishing for carving out the space for true voices to be heard, which falls completely in line with the book, and for having the courage and spunk to do so.

Ruth Bieber

Foreword

I am pleased to write a foreword to Ruth's book. She was a student and, later, a colleague in the Rehabilitation Studies Programme at the University of Calgary, and I have watched with interest her development and skills in life, drama and rehabilitation.

When I read the book draft, I became enthused and excited, for the material encompasses a number of strands, which she has carefully woven together. All these strands are topical and critical in understanding abilities and disabilities. At one level the book is her personal journey as a courageous woman who, though blind, met challenges that most of us do not ever have to face. At another level the book is a journey from disability to ability through the development of a drama company and, as its name implies, its aim was and is to turn things inside out. I like that because it deals with the formidable task of changing public and personal attitudes and approaches to disability through acting, and it does so creatively and constructively.

The book is a rigorous one, and is built on a philosophy of wellbeing and lives of quality for those who face challenges of one kind or another. It also has an international flavour. The approach is one that provides support when people face serious challenges. In this sense it is deeply humanitarian, accepting people and their challenges while promoting normal and inclusive behaviours. The book is also practical for it provides many and detailed examples of how to set up drama programs and companies in the context of disability, while regarding the people concerned as part of a normal continuum in society. Therefore, it represents an effective example of practice, which is at the demonstration edge of quality of life.

The book is also contemporary. It fits well with current research and practice in a worldwide move to enable people with challenges to strive for greater wellbeing, whether those challenges are physical, cognitive, or behavioural. It demonstrates, practically, how different aspects of life can be enhanced not just in acting, but also through drama, and effectively deals with the need to promote language, motor skills, friendship, and a host of other human skills and attributes. It is relevant to and can promote employment, health, and, critically, self-image.

Drama has long been underrated in terms of its life-building attributes. It tends to be seen by society as a frill when, in reality for many individuals, including those who are clearly disabled, as well as those who have less obvious challenges, it is an effective means of promoting opportunity, development, skill, and thus empowerment. These are the cornerstones for an effective civilization.

The book, in short, is inspiring and insightful. It is full of practical ideas and suggestions and should help individuals, those with and without disabilities, to build a more inclusive society.

Roy Brown, PhD
Professor Emeritus, University of Calgary, Canada, and
Emeritus Professor, Flinders University of South Australia

CHAPTER ONE

Overture

My name is Ruth Bieber, and I am the Artistic Director and Founder of the plucky, irreverent, non-traditional InsideOut Theatre in Calgary, Alberta in Canada. Since the early 1990s, my mission has involved Disability Theatre and Feminism. There is much to tell about my curvilinear journey through the evolution of my theatre company, but first, I must share a few pertinent details about myself.

I was not always Ruth Bieber. That is, I was for the first twenty-three years of my life, before I became Ruth Bieber-Something. I recall with clarity that mind numbing process of trying to decide what my married name should be. "Should I keep my maiden name, should I take my husband's surname, add a middle name, or should I go wild and make up a whole new name?" - a conundrum rarely experienced by men. The effort of coming to a decision, eventually made me realize that the drama surrounding being -"Something" was really, as the Bard would say "much ado about nothing." I might better have spent my mental energy on the important aspects of my new life: identity, finances, employment, education, and how married life could (and would) impact these critical parts of my world. More than eighteen years later, I am Ruth Bieber again.

So I ask myself: Why do women journey to find themselves, only to lose themselves when they become romantically involved. And, when that idea fails, once again embark on an arduous journey toward self-discovery? The great irony about this self-discovery is that it is familiar and authentic; the battle scars notwithstanding. Some choose to enter the cycle again. The jury is still out on me. I suspect, however, that I shall die at a ripe old age, and my name will still be Ruth Bieber. I am, at this moment, holding to that.

Don't get me wrong; those eighteen years were valuable. In fact, the years from 1983 – 1992 were particularly fruitful; during those years, I gave birth to two sons, worked full-time, and got my Master of Education degree specializing in Theatre and Disability. Those of you who have a similar chapter in your history know how much work is involved with that particular trio of events.

But wait. There is something else. Something that I don't always think about, something that many of my friends and working colleagues say they forget, and something that people, who meet me for the first time, say that they don't realise. Oh yes, that's right, now I remember. I am blind. My name is Ruth Bieber, I am the Artistic Director and Founder of the InsideOut Theatre Company, and I am blind.

I have found that this last revelation, met at first with a brief moment of amazement, is often followed by remarks which dismiss or minimize my accomplishments. Some even go on to dismiss me as a human being. I hear it in the comments that they make: "Your husband must really be a good housekeeper." Seriously? Or, "I'll bet your professors gave you lots of breaks." Sure, ever heard of "B" for blind? One of my favourites is, "Your children must really take care of you." Of course, don't all children ultimately raise their parents? Philosophy aside, make no mistake about it – I am their mother. Just ask them.

My favourite question is the inevitable: "When and how did you lose your vision?" This often causes me great dilemma because I am aware of the fact that at that moment - I am oddly, mysteriously, and unfairly representing every other blind person on earth, so I feel I should temper my response.

Ninety percent of the time, I manage to answer with eloquent cheerfulness, wearing a hat that says, "I am here to educate and exercise self advocacy." My well-rehearsed monologue begins with, "I have two children; a Master's degree; am gainfully employed with my own theatre company," and the punch line: "I am one of the happiest people you will ever meet." There, I said it. Because I know it is important to say, even though I suspect it is met with disbelief.

I know there is disbelief when a second question follows: Can't the doctors do something?" "Like what?" I confess that I am tempted to say: "Provide me with a special device that ensures I never have to have this weary conversation again." But no, I say nothing, and try to change the subject. The other ten percent of the time, my response might be something like this: "I lost my sight very suddenly at the absolute best time to go blind – when I was young enough to adjust easily, yet old enough to retain a wonderfully imaginative visual memory." Or I might say, "I'll tell you when I went blind if you tell me when you lost your virginity." The other standard question is, "Why did you go blind?" My classic reply is, "Just lucky I guess." These responses may seem impertinent, but they are no less important than the purely educational ones. Sometimes an unexpected or humorous response goes a long way toward the deconstruction of assumptions.

We've all been there. No one knows everything about other people all the time. It's whether we choose to humble ourselves in order to change an attitude. I believe in change; I believe in self-expression, and I believe in individuality. This is no doubt why I am the Artistic Director and originator of a non-traditional theatre company. Even though I had never actually given myself the title...Until...

It was January 2001. I had just completed the two-year process of shedding the 'status' of being someone's 'wife' (now there's an oxymoron) and I was looking forward to participating in The High Performance Rodeo, a theatre festival in Calgary. I was sitting at my kitchen table with Katherine Duncan from CBC Radio. As she interviewed me, she made inquiries about the theatre company and our participation in the festival. That's when it happened. She looked at me and asked, more as a statement than a question, "So, you're the Artistic Director of InsideOut Theatre?"

And there it was, one of those life-altering moments that surprises with a revelation of what was there all along, but not recognized or acknowledged. I looked at her and wondered if she saw it in my eyes, that brief pause in which an entire lifetime stands between us. Less than a second passed, but it felt like an eternity. I remember thinking, "I hadn't thought of myself as a person with a title." and I was instantly transported, ironically, to another time in my life when I had mysteriously lost my vision.

I am seven years old, and I am sitting on the side of a hospital bed waiting for what turned out to be the first of two exploratory brain surgeries. My father is standing next to me. He is diligently completing a questionnaire. He does not know yet that the surgeries are merely exploratory and not really designed to restore my vision. That realisation came later, after my second surgery. So, for the time being, he is attentive and hopeful. He knows the answers to most of the questions and does not really involve me. Suddenly I hear him read, "Does your child suck his/her thumb?" He alters his gaze from the form to my face and says, "Well?" It is that same question/statement/question pattern. Katherine Duncan and my father are both looking at me and waiting. I am looking back and realising that neither of them will wait long, so in my mind, I deeply bend my knees, and jump. It is liberating to let go of everything you ever thought you knew. I say, "No, I do not suck my thumb," and "Yes, I am the Artistic Director." In both instances, I experienced the power of spontaneity and the realisation that it's all in the power of the words.

Upon reflection, I realise that in both cases, those important transformations were relatively easy. In the former case, I simply redirected my focus from thumbs – I was ambidextrous – to the rest of my fingers. I became a merciless nail biter, often rendering my fingers raw and bleeding. I probably should have remained with the comfort of thumb sucking, as the nail biting took decades to kick. But I stopped sucking my thumb.

In the latter instance, the transformation was far less dramatic. After all, for the previous seven years, I had been moulding, fund-raising, developing, obtaining non-profit and charitable status, mentoring, teaching, acting, producing, promoting, hiring, supervising, and the list continues. Anyone who has built her or his own theatre company from scratch knows it is an extraordinary labour of love. And the fact remains: I was and still am, at the time of this writing, the Artistic Director of InsideOut Theatre. I simply had not said it out loud in that way before.

Time and again, throughout my life, I have realised the creative potential of the spoken word. If we say it is so, then typically one of three situations follows:

1.   It is the truth.

2.   It becomes the truth because we take action to make it the truth.

3.   It is not the truth, but we remain steeped in denial and self-justification and continue to insist on it being truth.

In life and in theatre, I have experienced these variations countless times. Fundamentally, it is all in the name. My name is Ruth Bieber, and I am the Artistic Director and Founder of InsideOut Theatre Company, and that is my truth. Easy to say...

Disability Theatre, Feminism, and Leslie Fanelli

Before proceeding, it is important to explore the definitions of Disability Theatre and Feminism as each relates directly to the InsideOut experience. Disability Theatre as performed by the InsideOut Theatre Company is 'original' theatre where actors with various disabilities both create and perform for all types of audiences. These original, colourful theatre pieces emanate from improvisational acting based on a specific topic, for example, school days, the family portrait, or employment. Eventually, these improvised scripts become somewhat frozen or scripted. While there are certain key points that must remain true to the scripted topic in performance, there remains ample improvisational leeway. The non-traditional casting at InsideOut includes a few actors without disabilities, performing alongside the featured actors with disabilities.

The rehearsal process for the InsideOut Theatre is virtually the opposite of rehearsal for traditional theatre. Traditional theatre is where the actor moulds him/ herself into a pre-determined role whereas, our process focuses on the specific talents and circumstances of each performer. For example, one actor communicates entirely non-verbally due to a brain injury, and all her scenes include this unique ability- likewise, for a performer with quadriplegia or one who uses a walker or cane. All circumstances are included in rehearsal, resulting in unique performances that best present each person's talents, abilities and disabilities. Yes, disabilities are front and centre; we have Disability Pride! At InsideOut, we do not embrace covert or overt 'ableism', which means, according to the *Merriam Webster Online Dictionary*, "Discrimination or prejudice against individuals with disabilities— able·ist □ *adjective.*" More aptly described by the online dictionary *Wiktionary* (created of, by, and for the people) the definition of 'ableism' is, "Discrimination against people with disabilities in favour of able-bodied people. The belief that people with disabilities are inferior to others. Etymology: From *able* + *-ism*, patterned on _racism_, _sexism_, and _heterosexism_ in meaning."

Disability and theatre are united uniquely at InsideOut. With traditional theatre, performers and creators with disabilities can be onstage, featured in a traditional showcase or workshop, or merely in the audience. In a blatant display of ableism, people with disabilities are sometimes the focus onstage, acted by performers without disabilities. None of this is the same as Disability Theatre at InsideOut, where our specific, original improvisational style highlights performers and creators with disabilities in original productions, featuring an inclusive cast, for inclusive audiences.

The mission of InsideOut Theatre is to level the theatrical playing field (and the playing field of life) for performers and creators with disabilities. Our goal is to enable participants with disabilities to participate in, enjoy, and benefit from creative drama training.

Inherent in this mission is the ensuing definition of 'Feminism'. Feminism is the process of accommodating and elevating the environment in a cooperative and mutually beneficial manner in order to promote maximum and respectful participation in the domain of choice for _all_ members of society. Feminism highlights the equality of women. Men, as well as women, can be Feminists. As such, everybody wins.

After the completion of the first draft of this book, I met a creative Feminist, who also has a theatre company similar to InsideOut. It was via the Internet that I first encountered Leslie Fanelli, Artistic Director and Founder of Theatre in Motion in the Greater New York City area. Some of the original productions at Theatre in Motion were developed in the same manner as InsideOut productions, and all Theatre in Motion productions involve creators and performers with and without disabilities. Leslie herself deals with bipolar disorder and dyslexia, and uses a hearing aid. She is a Disability Rights and Disability Pride activist via theatre arts. Not surprisingly, we became fast friends, and when I moved to New York City, she assisted me enormously, with her detailed editorial contributions. Although this book is about the InsideOut Theatre Company, her input as a like-minded theatre artist remains valuable to me and is in artistic tandem with my non-traditional theatre philosophy. In fact, worthy of note: in the early 1990s, while InsideOut was embryonic in Western Canada, in synchronicity, Theatre in Motion was also emerging, unbeknownst to me, on the East Coast of the United States. This phenomenon lends credibility to the value of the Disability Theatre movement on a global scale.

Before proceeding a note regarding terminology is warranted. Currently there is much debate with respect to terminology as it relates to people (actors) with disabilities. Personally, I prefer the less cumbersome and politically powerful term disabled actor, or more specifically where relevant, blind actor, Deaf actor, etc. Having said this, I have for numerous reasons and for the most part, chosen to use the phrase, 'actor with a disability and so on. The reasons for this choice are complicated, and not the focus of this book. The comment is made here for its own sake; that is the recognition of many and varied perspectives. Each perspective is legitimate in its own right. Also, a note regarding the capitalization of the word 'Deaf'; while potentially confusing from a literary perspective, is intentional and serves a political agenda for some members of the Deaf community.

Basic Principles and Practical Applications

The information that follows is critical in understanding Disability Theatre. It includes six initial guiding principles, important concepts, and practical applications that are foundational to InsideOut Theatre and Theatre in Motion.

Principle One: Artistic expression is intrinsic to the human experience and fundamental to maintaining individual and societal balance.

Principle Two: It is the right of each person, whether it is a colourful bold finger painting of a young child or the polished performance of a seasoned opera singer, to fully express herself.

Principle Three: Any artistic experience can be adapted to accommodate the idiosyncrasies and creative abilities of any artist, and limitations to this end come only as a result of a lack of willingness or imagination. At InsideOut, the majority of the artists[1] face challenges in their ability to read, write, verbalise, and/or memorise. For this reason, the InsideOut rehearsal process is virtually opposite to that of mainstream theatre. As briefly noted, in theatre, the actor is typically required to mould into a predetermined part at an audition, hopefully to be cast for this part in a prepared script. InsideOut Theatre, however, shapes the rehearsal and the ultimate performance to accommodate each actor's strengths and abilities. I recall one actor who could only respond with the word, "Yes." Hence, his performance pieces centred entirely on his ability to say, "Yes." This

---

[1] InsideOut participants often consider themselves theatre artists and/or actors first and group participants, second. Hence, I also refer to them as artists, although I sometimes use interchangeably actors, participants, and performers. With our improvisational style, the performers are also, in part, creators of the InsideOut theatre presentations.

strategy was so successful that during one season, a complete show was built around this ability. I will never forget how thrilled this actor was to be the star of the production.

A second strategy used by InsideOut Theatre is to involve actors in 'rehearsed improvisation'. Productions based on the true-life experiences of the artists (giving their stories voice and visibility) are developed and rehearsed. Without the use of written scripts, vignettes are repeated until they become second nature and ritualistic, while remaining fresh in performance. Delivered in a believable, conversational manner, the real-life stories have specific literary points that are highlighted during stage delivery. These have been coached and finessed by the director: a beginning, middle, denouement, ending, and theme, all of which are derived naturally during rehearsal.

Before moving on to Principle Four, a note regarding inclusion is necessary. It could be argued that a segregated program, even in part, is not inclusive in nature. The InsideOut Theatre process, however, holds the belief that people with disabilities can learn just as much, if not more, from one another as from people without disabilities. Inclusion comes with the theatrical experience itself, rather than the ratio of individuals with differing abilities, and there are usually a minority of performers without disabilities in each production. Furthermore, because theatre is noted for its consciousness-raising impact on society: inclusion is fostered.

Principle Four: Creativity is emotional in nature and an expression of the soul: subsequently, great care is given to the respectful treatment of each of the actors and their contribution to the process. InsideOut actors are tireless in their dedication and contribution to the collective creation. This is a natural consequence of being treated with consideration and respect, as valued members of InsideOut. Actors are frequently heard saying, "When I came to rehearsal this morning I was feeling sad and lethargic, but now I feel uplifted and energised!"[2]

Principle Five: The experience should be enjoyable. The enjoyment factor relates directly to the skills of InsideOut facilitators, individuals trained to work with populations with (and sometimes without) disabilities during the theatrical process. It is the responsibility of the Artistic Director to train the facilitators, who essentially serve as assistant directors. With practice, we all learn the value of building success into each rehearsal and production, fortified by the power of laughter. In its inception, InsideOut Theatre did not intend to develop humorous productions. Rather, humour was a natural evolution that came directly out of the desire to create a safe and enjoyable atmosphere for the actors. Over time, InsideOut audiences have come to expect a show that will make them laugh. The motto has become, "Our message is serious, but our delivery is humorous." The rehearsal process culminating in performance is so safe and enjoyable that no one escapes its lure. I recall a support worker who participated with InsideOut Theatre only because she was hired to accompany a protégé with disabilities. This support worker was considered a most shy individual by her friends and family. Before long, however, this same worker was seen playing her guitar and singing a performance opening solo. Her friends and family viewed this in a state of disbelief: "How did you get her onstage?" they asked. I responded, "That's what humour, mutual respect, and gentle encouragement get you."

Principle Six: In keeping with Howard Gardner's *Theory of Multiple Intelligences* (MI), we believe that art is also cognitive in nature. The emotional aspects of the work at

---

[2] Statement is a paraphrase as it was stated in various ways at various times depending on the verbal ability of the speaker. This paraphrased statement brings to mind the famous early twentieth century painter, Kandinsky, who said that "Art is the expression of the soul."

InsideOut are based on the *Personal Intelligences*: these being interpersonal, intrapersonal, and linguistic Intelligence.

Following is a typical rehearsal session at InsideOut Theatre, which embodies the aforementioned six principles:

1. Rehearsals are typically 1.5 hours in duration in order to accommodate the limited concentration span of some actors. To support the actors, facilitators will refer to specific previously established ground rules, if things get off track. Rehearsals begin with a 'check in', where facilitators actively listen to the comments of the actors and create balance by establishing a time limit of three minutes per actor. To maximise concentration, actors' concerns must be heard and responded to, if possible, within the three minute time limit. Furthermore, facilitators are aware that for many artists with disabilities, being 'present' requires intense focus and fortitude. After the artists have endured the challenges of their morning routines and transportation, this opening 'check in' establishes a short, sweet transition into rehearsal. Listening and speaking are equally important, so that actors with disabilities learn from one another. This successful practise challenges popular theories of inclusion which discourage people with disabilities from gathering as an empowered group. Inclusion theories promote assimilation into "normal", non-disabled populations which can result in 'ableism'.

2. A theme is established collectively during an initial session. The theme is discussed and each actor shares a personal response to this theme. Facilitators take notes and consider ideas with respect to the production. Once again, the discussion is limited, with the facilitator (assistant director) gently reminding the group that there will be future opportunities for discussion. Facilitators explain that the purpose of the gathering is to create theatre not an encounter group.

3. With encouragement, the actors then explore the space, their bodies, their voices, and their emotions. Many exercise manuals, some of which are included in the Book List, are available to stimulate ideas for activities. Facilitators must remember that adaptations are welcome and limited only by the imagination and by the willingness of the group members.

4. Once the creative juices have been stimulated, and the group has been energised, facilitators break the actors into well-balanced small groups of three or four, and begin developing scenes using the information gathered in the theme discussion. Week to week, the rehearsed improvisations become increasingly more polished and refined. Between the weekly sessions, facilitators debrief past rehearsals and plan for upcoming ones. Production ideas and suggestions are discussed and then brought to the next rehearsal for collective input. In my experience, weekly rehearsals are manageable for individuals whose transportation needs are challenging and whose lives are generally complex.

5. At the end of each rehearsal, facilitators make a few closing remarks, and each actor is given the opportunity to talk about what he or she did or did not enjoy that day.

Perhaps one of the most important doctrines guiding InsideOut Theatre's process stems from its 'a-scriptive' rather than 'pre-scriptive' philosophy. In other words, strengths are ascribed positively to the actors: identification and focus on deficits is avoided. In this way Insideout does not respond to limitations with prescriptive measures. This process is based on the belief that there are no wrong answers, only creative solutions. Facilitators are not viewed as specialists who prescribe treatments based on diagnostics. They do not focus on areas of deficit by attempting to eliminate or mask the challenge. Moreover, reframing the initially perceived shortfall as a potential theatrical contribution frequently leads to creative outcome.

The 'pre-scriptive' approach, sometimes referred to as the Medical Model does, in my experience, hold one important piece of value. Actors with disabilities often possess a myriad of medical conditions. These must be documented, with appropriate strategic preparation to ensure the safety and well-being of all; behavioural management plans should be in place to be implemented if needed. For example, the actor with *retinitis pigmentosa* perceives the world through a narrow tunnel. People with tunnel vision often appear to be fully sighted because central vision controls detailed sight. It is only when the actor crashes over a low-lying stage prop that the vision disability becomes apparent. Potential injuries can easily be avoided with awareness and understanding of medical conditions.

Another example is the actor with epilepsy. As there are many different types of seizure, which require different responses; it is important to be knowledgeable. The 'a-scriptive' principle therefore, does not ignore disabling conditions; rather in true improvisational form, it accepts them as part of the theatrical offering, building them into the production. A unique doctrine that guides the InsideOut process is that of mediation between the internal and external realities by transcending traditional verbal approaches. In other words, we transcend the typical behaviour of talking and talking and talking with the more right-brained response of sparking the imagination followed by action. One of my favourite examples is witnessing an actor with Tourette Syndrome whose symptoms disappeared when he was in character on stage. When someone is deep in their imagination, which an actor must be, the right brain is involved, freeing the mind from left brain's hesitations and ticks. As the blind Artistic Director of an integrated theatre company, transcending verbal approaches has been my greatest personal challenge.

Many of our actors possess physical verbal, and/or intellectual challenges that result in articulation difficulties. As an individual who is blind, I rely heavily on speech and other audible cues. My goal is to understand the individual actors in as much depth and detail as possible: 'Know thy actor,' has been my credo. Relying on the feedback and expertise of co-facilitators and community supports has helped me personally and aided in the success of the InsideOut process. I recall an actor with a hearing impairment, who joined the company in its early years. I was a little dubious but he was determined and passionate, to say the least. After two seasons of theatre training, it became obvious that he could benefit from a sign language interpreter. It wasn't I who was resistant to the idea: the problem was that, although he knew sign language, he was suspicious of anyone who was part of the Deaf Community. Finally he was convinced, and a sign language interpreter was hired. As a result, communication improved immeasurably. For actors with other types of communication challenges, physical and/or vocal theatrical training can lead to rich and exciting theatre.

As the Company offers several creative theatre-training programs, artists are afforded on-going choice within the theatrical arena. Actors who are involved with the training workshops can develop their skill level in preparation for taking on the rigors of the InsideOut touring group. On the other hand, there are some actors who, after several years with the touring group, decide to step back and rejoin one of the less rigorous programs. Regardless of the choice of the actor, involvement with InsideOut Theatre offers skill development which is not only specific to the theatre but also generalises to the greater community.

Many InsideOut actors have been able to secure employment or volunteer positions in the community based on skills learned at InsideOut. Salient skills include speech and listening skills, increased attention and concentration, improved interpersonal relations, improved self-awareness, positive self-concept, body awareness, improved physical movement, and increased self-confidence and self-esteem. Moreover, artists and facilitators alike find the involvement with InsideOut Theatre an enjoyable experience that consistently promotes laughter, creativity, and a sense of belonging.

All artistic expressions aim to promote left and right brain communication. This is achieved by two means. Primarily by utilizing drama games and activities that cross the midline of the brain by accessing both hemispheres, such as Liar's Tag (see full description below); second by accessing right brain functioning within a predominantly left brain culture /context. What is meant by this? There are five symbol systems that we use in the process of learning: words, numbers, sounds, images, and gestures. Except for specialised educational opportunities, words and numbers continue to dominate the classroom, and this effectively minimises a vast array of teaching and learning strategies.

Participation in extracurricular activities of an artistic nature promotes balance and emotional well-being for all. Theatre Arts are no exception. Hence, participation with InsideOut Theatre inherently promotes balance and a sense of well-being for its actors. Even activities that initially pose a challenge can become rehearsal favourites over time. A good example is an activity called 'Liar's Tag'. In this game a group of actors stand in a circle. The first actor performs an action, for example, brushing his teeth. The second actor asks "What are you doing?" and the first actor responds by lying, claiming a different action, such as cleaning a toilet. The second actor then must act out the lie of cleaning the toilet. The third actor in the circle then asks "What are you doing?" The toilet cleaner then responds with yet another lie which the third actor must copy, and then lie about. The actions and lies continue around the circle. This initially challenging right brain/left brain activity has become a favourite for InsideOut actors. Audiences also enjoy this theatre exercise of juxtaposition, which is often hilarious.

InsideOut Theatre Fundamentals

Rehearsed Improvisation

No two InsideOut performances are exactly the same; however they maintain a consistency of theme and presentation. To maintain the integrity of any performance, some vignette fragments must remain consistent, where other parts may lend themselves to spontaneity and freedom of expression. The directors and facilitators become skilled in distinguishing one from the other, and in identifying the appropriate placement of each.

The rehearsed/improvisational process promotes freedom of expression and adds an element of security, since the actors have a good idea of what is coming next. A rehearsed improvisational model also works well for actors who are unable to read or memorise the printed word. Any particular scene is simply rehearsed as many times as needed to memorise the inflexible parts. When a script is too loose, the meanings can dissolve, so memorization of some fragments is necessary.

Choosing a Theme

Any theme chosen by InsideOut artists must fundamentally support the actors' right to creative expression. Through the exploration of the chosen theme, a sense of personal and collective authenticity emerges. Is this the "magic of theatre"? Perhaps not in the sense of mainstream theatre arts: but the unfolding of authenticity, as it relates to creative expression, can certainly be theatrical and magical. Ideally, the group chooses a theme collectively, and then explores that theme using the life experiences of the actors in the group. Since the artists have an opportunity to share their unique experiences as they relate to the theme, commonalities among group members emerge. Validation results from this process, and when various situations are shared, the outcome is rich with perspective. Becoming aware of another person's point of view by acting it out promotes individual growth, greater understanding within a community, and ultimately social change. When properly facilitated, any theme holds the potential for drawing individual stories together, and creating a cohesive whole.

It is possible for a program funder to dictate a theme. On the surface, this may seem less than ideal; nevertheless, we are open to funder's suggestions because any theme can promote the actors' creativity and authentic expression.

Tableaux

Since the inaugural InsideOut performance, tableaux have been used in rehearsals and performances. Tableaux, serve as an excellent exploratory theatrical activity in a rehearsal. Having actors pose as human statues helps to demonstrate a concept or idea. In performance, tableaux provide an effective means of introducing a performance or act. A tableau tells the audience the theme and what the actors think and feel about the theme.

The typical tableau rehearsal process is as follows:

1.   After the group of actors has established a theme, interesting aspects of it are explored through the use of tableau.

2.   All the actors sit in a performance line[3] facing the audience, directly in front of the curtain or backdrop. (If a curtain or backdrop is not available, the performance line

---

[3] A performance line is a minimalist theatrical strategy used to separate the audience from the performers and consists of a row of chairs where a backdrop would be, and where actors sit facing the audience when not performing.

itself acts as an upstage indicator.)

3.   From this group of seated actors, one actor is chosen to declare the theme, for example "Belonging."

4.   This actor moves forward into the acting area and declares the theme with drama and bravado. Then the actor freezes in position.

5.   Each actor in turn attaches to those who have gone before, and also freezes in position. The new actor contributes a personal association to the theme and calls it out, again with drama and bravado. For example, an associative addition to the theme "Belonging" might be "Friendship."

6.   Once all the actors have attached themselves to the frozen arrangement of figures, one actor quietly says, "On the count of three. One. Two. Three!" The entire group then enthusiastically announces the theme in unison "Belonging!" The use of tableaux, like the use of humour, has become a tradition with InsideOut performances.

Vignettes

The vignette as a production modality has consistently proven valuable to InsideOut. A vignette can be presented alone, as opposed to a scene which is usually a component of a complete performance. For both practical and theatrical reasons, performing vignettes with a common theme has become an InsideOut tradition. Vignettes permit a performance to fit within a specified time frame. For example, four vignettes could constitute one half-hour workshop performance, while twelve vignettes could serve as banquet entertainment for a conference. Vignettes of a similar theme can be cut from or added to shows easily.

The flexibility of the vignette helps us keep our performance commitments. Due to the often fragile nature of our actors, it is not uncommon to receive a telephone call days or even hours before a performance reporting an artist's regret. I recall receiving that fateful phone call once, an hour before a fringe festival performance. A support worker told me that one of our key actors had fallen ill. Immediately, I turned to the ready performers and announced "regroup," which they did, and, indeed, the show went on successfully.

Another advantage of the vignette lies in performance equity. For each actor, there is the possibility of starring in a single vignette, which typically lasts about fifteen minutes. Artists with memory deficits or different learning abilities may not be up to the challenge of a major role for an entire performance, yet take delight in starring in one or two vignettes.

Finally, vignettes permit greater role flexibility and a variety of character building opportunities. Since actors with disabilities often find themselves in limiting life circumstances, being onstage offers a spectrum of parts to be played. Actors can experiment and enjoy as they try on new personas.

There must be some caution and awareness on the part of facilitators. A fine balance needs to be maintained between actor input and public perception. The vignette *Don't Feed the Ducks* is an excellent case in point. During rehearsal, actors were enthusiastically willing to play the part of rather comical and misbehaved ducks. Within the disability culture, however, this might have caused offence, since it suggested an association between adults with disabilities and animals. I was uncomfortable with this vignette and expressed concerns. The actors outvoted me, and the vignette was performed to the great delight of audiences. Conversely, in the vignette *The Hearing Dog*, it was suggested that an actor play the Hearing Dog. In this case, I vetoed the suggestion, as I was certain a miming technique would avoid negative connotations while conveying the message just as effectively. This turned out to be a good choice.

Between Vignette Fillers

When working with actors with disabilities, the process of play development slows to accommodate various learning styles. As InsideOut performances evolved and the vignettes grew more elaborate, the need for creative connectors between vignettes became apparent. These fillers allow an appropriate pace and provide entertainment for the audience during vignette changes. Examples of useful fillers include corresponding song fragments, songs sung by a small group of actors, poetry readings, a simulated talk show, or a school bell shrilling out. The list is endless, limited only by the imagination.

The first InsideOut performance, *Belonging*, used the simple but classic technique of costume change. In each vignette, the person who did not belong wore a green T-shirt. The other characters, who did belong, wore red. The audience soon began to understand, and the vignette changes were simple and quick.

Choosing a Title

Ideally, the title of any performance is catchy and/or artistically pleasing. Examples of titles from the scripts presented in this book include *Belonging*; *Work, Work, Work*; *School Days*; *The Family Portrait; Advocacy in Action*; *Millennium Dreams*; *Help Unwanted*; and *Maestropiece Theatre*.

Theme Song

A theme song, sung and signed, accentuates both the theatrical and the integrative nature of InsideOut Theatre. Presenting the song in sign language is simple and also varies the presentation. Initially, the theme song was sung onstage by two actors playing guitars. Later, the entire group sang with guitar accompaniment provided by a sound system. Most recently, the theme song was delivered without musical accompaniment, but in concert with an upbeat foot-stomping, hand-clapping rhythm. This latest development has been most challenging for the actors who are required to sing, sign, and keep rhythm simultaneously. Not all actors have mastered this combination of skills, but consistent practice has proved to be well worth the effort.

The InsideOut song:

We are climbing a ladder to a better way,

We are fighting each day for our rights,

Everyone stand up and shout,

We are InsideOut!

Closing Chant

Several expressions of the pride and camaraderie that develop among InsideOut performers are evident, but none more so than the closing InsideOut chant. At the end of each rehearsal, performance, or workshop, one of the participants declares, "And together we're...?" The enthusiastic, energetic, and united response is, "InsideOut!"

Costuming and Properties

True to the minimalist approach of the InsideOut practice, costuming and properties (props) remain simple. Costumes consist of black pants, black socks, black shoes, and a coloured T-shirt which corresponds to the performance theme. (Be aware that red, while a vibrant and theatrical colour, tends to bleed on video recordings.) T-shirt designs range from professional to amateur, depending on budget and artist availability. Simple costumes make the transition from rehearsal to performance run smoothly.

Extra black socks and T-shirts should be available, to ensure the uniformity of theatrical presentation. Actors often require countless reminders to attend to details which, if forgotten, result in problems. This is a reality for all actors, not just actors with disabilities. I recall a performance where a facilitator/performer arrived in blue jeans and grey socks. In the collaborative atmosphere of InsideOut Theatre, the other members of the company brought this to my attention, and the facilitator was asked to change her clothes to conform to the general standard of black pants and socks.

With respect to props, our motto is "Less is more." Fewer props help accommodate budgetary restraints, make transportation easier, and result in less clutter and confusion onstage. This does not mean the stage is devoid of props. A few carefully chosen, easy-to-manage props facilitate connection with the audience. A simple mask or well-placed prop can speak volumes.

On rare occasions, actors have made the request for more elaborate costumes and additional props. While these requests are always seriously considered, the principle remains – use props sparsely to convey information to the audience. A fine and delicate balance exists between too few and too many props. Too few, and the audience is left distracted and puzzled. Too many, and the actors with spatial and memory deficits have difficulty. If there is too much to think about, the flow of the performance can be jeopardised.

Number of Participants

As InsideOut Theatre grew, programs began to expand to accommodate varying abilities and commitment levels. It became apparent that the number of participants in each group needed to be considered. The Touring Group, for example, has become smaller in number, consisting of recruited actors and compatible actor/facilitators in a ratio of one to one (a total cast of no more than ten or twelve members). Non-touring groups continue to enjoy larger numbers of participant/actors, with fewer actor/facilitators or support partners (the total number of actors can reach as high as twenty or thirty per group).

Actor compatibility within each group is also important, but close friendships and/or romantic partnerships can be disruptive. As Artistic Director, a most difficult challenge arises when having to ask an actor to leave a group due to relationship issues.

A note about the scripts: The scripts in this book are not polished; rather, they are loosely formatted to serve as templates that can be revised to reflect the individual taste and desire of any group. I trust they will be as enjoyable to read as they were to develop and perform.

CHAPTER TWO

Feminism, Disability, Shamanism, and Theatre Arts

I made the connection between Disability Theatre and Feminism in the mid-1980s when I was taking graduate courses in both subjects.[4] To my mind, the parallels were unmistakable. Interestingly, though, my studies in Feminism made no reference to either Disability or Theatre, and the course in Disability Theatre Arts did not breathe a word about Feminism. Was I the only one who saw these parallels? By definition, broadly conceived Feminism embraces diversity and individual expression. Feminism desires to elevate the status of minority and disadvantaged populations, and challenge the status quo. Like Feminism, Disability Theatre fundamentally encourages all people to express themselves creatively and dramatically. My own evolution as a Feminist and theatre artist combined with the evolution of the company; provide a unique example of the way in which these streams of thought come together.

Subsequent to my original epiphany, I discovered another powerful connection between performance and the healing arts; namely Shamanism (as comprehensively described in Rogan P. Taylor's book *The Death and Resurrection Show: From Shaman to Superstar*). Ironically, this book was published in 1985, coinciding precisely with my original insights about the nurturing, all inclusive nature of Disability Theatre and Feminism. Black Elk, an Oglala Sioux Shaman, is quoted in Taylor's book: "A man (woman) who has a vision is not able to use the power of it until after he has performed

---

[4] Note that much of this chapter is drawn directly from my article, The Truth about Theatre from the InsideOut, printed in *Canadian Theatre Review* 122 (2005).

the vision on earth for the people to see."[5] The therapeutic nature of creating and performing an original theatre piece becomes complete in inclusive sharing with an audience, which is an artistic expression of Feminism. Disability Theatre, as performed by InsideOut, is equally nurturing and embracing. Hence, the links between Shamanism, Feminism, and Disability Theatre are clearly illustrated.

In that global spirit, I prefer to use the pronouns 'she' or 'her,' interchanged with the male pronouns 'he' or 'him'. So, too, will I sometimes substitute 'man' with 'woman,' as an integral Feminist representation of my text. This is not some sort of word game; let's face it, the paramount power of words has changed history and its interpretation, and in no small way, leads the world today. Since InsideOut stresses flexibility in its creative endeavours, it makes perfect sense to utilize feminine and masculine pronouns. Naturally, many InsideOut roles can be played interchangeably with equal authenticity by a woman or man.

InsideOut Theatre defines a fully inclusive spirit and was incorporated in 1996. The company received charitable status in 1997, with the mandate to provide theatre training and performing opportunities to people with disabilities. The incorporation process began in the fall of 1994. During these early days, innocence and naiveté, coupled with the great enthusiasm from the collective, created a sense that everything was possible. Although I was aware that both Feminism and Disability were controversial, for the most part, I rarely saw this as an obstacle. I did become acutely aware, however, that our unorthodox drama practice challenged the mainstream theatre community.

In the early nineties, I had the opportunity to do something called Drama Therapy, but its focus was more on therapy than on drama, and the presence of a psychiatrist and/or

---

[5] *Death and Resurrection Show*, p. 9.

related professional was required. When a colleague suggested I shift from the therapeutic setting into the community, I was willing to give it a shot.

The sheer power of performance quickly seduced me,[6] and slowly, but with great enthusiasm from the collective, InsideOut Theatre began to take on a life of its own. Now, many years later, theatre for people with disabilities flourishes internationally, in a multiplicity of fascinating formats.

I learned about VSA from Leslie Fanelli who, in addition to running her non-traditional company, Theatre in Motion, worked for VSA New Jersey. She was also involved with VSA New York, VSA South Africa, and Accessible Arts in Australia. VSA is the 'International Organization on Arts and Disabilities,' an affiliate of the John F. Kennedy Centre for the Performing Arts, located in Washington, DC. VSA embraces Vision, Strength, and Artistic Expression. Its mission is to provide arts and education opportunities for people with disabilities and to increase access to the arts for all.

There are VSA affiliates all over the United States, and a multiplicity of affiliates worldwide, including two Canadian affiliates, Ontario and Quebec. This broad-based, much esteemed organization celebrates the totality of music, dance, visual art, literary arts, and theatre arts in the lives of people with disabilities. This organization of like-minded spirit includes only one actual theatre company (The Unlimited Potential Theatre Company), a project of VSA New Jersey.

---

[6] Taylor colourfully points out that in addition to a Shaman possessing medical skills, he worked in the "context of a magical performance…producing a similar ecstatic condition in everyone gathered for the occasion" (p. 41).

In addition to VSA, a search on the Internet will reveal exciting Disability Theatre presented in ways similar, comparable, and dissimilar to production styles at InsideOut. The National Arts Disability Centre serves as a huge directory of Arts and Disabilities organisations in the USA. In Canada, there are two notable directories: The Society of Disability Arts and Culture and Ryerson University's Institute for Disability Studies, Research and Education. A number of arts organizations are listed in these directories but of long standing credit are Glenvale Players and Out of Sight Productions in Ontario, Theatre Terrific in Vancouver , and Long Side Players on the Canadian east coast. I share this overview with you to show that Disability Theatre is a vibrant grassroots movement. Paradoxically, in spite of its evident vitality, Disability Theatre remains largely marginalised from mainstream theatre and audiences.

Traditional theatre tends to promote the myth that creativity and artistic expression are the domain of a few elite, talented individuals, while the philosophical premise underlying Disability Theatre à la InsideOut promotes the creative and artistic rights of all individuals. Creativity is, after all, inherent in everyone. [7] We are all creative beings, regardless of whether we receive payment for our creations.

InsideOut Theatre began with a focus on individuals with a variety of disabling conditions: physical, developmental, behavioural, sensory, and mental health. A related interesting phenomenon occurred as the project evolved. Many people with disabilities who were referred to the company came with support partners, professionals hired to provide assistance in a variety of capacities. These professionals were not necessarily interested in theatre arts, but by virtue of their position, were required to participate.

---

[7] Interestingly, Taylor describes candidates for the position of Shaman as often sickly, moody, lonely and, fundamentally, dreamers or visionaries (p.24).

Many became and continue to be enthusiastic and willing performers in spite of initial trepidation. Their continued involvement is clear evidence that our theatrical process is both safe and inclusive: a cooperative of equal members, with different yet compatible abilities.

One inherent challenge with the notion of equality is that checks and balances must constantly be designed, reinforced, and redesigned. Equality means upholding the collective agreement that no lead actor is in charge, or more important than any other. Rather, we are all responsible for the success of the cooperative theatrical endeavour. A keen and heartfelt sense of responsibility towards the collective is naturally felt or understood by some more deeply than by others. For example, an actor with a brain injury may have difficulty with time management. Other InsideOut actors would understand his actions as lack of ability rather than lack of cooperative spirit. Rarely does this support exist in mainstream theatre; but in Disability Theatre, those who do not assume responsibility of a practical nature still contribute by offering their trust and willingness. What each participant brings to the table is valued and respected. Obviously, without the actors with disabilities, there would be no company. The lines between participants are further blurred because everyone (the actors with disabilities, support workers and facilitators) contributes unique life experiences to the performance theme. At InsideOut we build on strengths and abilities rather than focus on deficits and disabilities. That is, instead of seeing deficiencies and excluding what does not work, we strive to see abilities, and find ways to make everything work.

Our model draws from Feminist theory in two ways. It embodies Susan Gubar's observation that "women's creativity is prior to literacy"[8] by using the rehearsal process as the creative cauldron from which the production is formed.

---

[8] "The Blank Page" and the Issues of Female Creativity, p. 259.

Our model also fits well with the weblike mentality towards human connection described in Carol Gilligan's *In a Different Voice*. Gilligan's book highlights the differences in moral and cognitive development between men and women. She proposes that men tend to be linear, rendering them more focused and single-minded; thus, less able to multi-task or engage in the cooperative. Conversely, women see themselves as an integral part of a weblike societal structure and are inherently inclusive in their approaches to community living. This nonlinear, inclusive approach underlies every InsideOut production.

Women and people with disabilities experience 'ghettoisation', and like the performers in Disability Theatre collectives, women have been able to participate in patriarchal society only if they conform to its expectations. If they fail to conform—women, and people with disabilities find themselves relegated to second-class venues, supporting roles, and inferior job opportunities. Theatre, like patriarchal culture, has held fast to the misconception that if you put actors with disabilities or women into traditional roles, all will be well. This philosophy does not represent a genuine inclusiveness that embraces diversity. It is more accurately another form of the patriarchy. With Disability Theatre, all interested actors and other participants (support partners) have equal opportunity to perform.

At InsideOut Theatre, we educate, we advocate, and we inspire actors and audience members to believe in their own creative abilities. As the second-wave of Feminists discovered, it is not enough to raise the consciousness of individual women. For society to evolve, it is necessary to alter perceptions of women and men at every level. In the same way, InsideOut Theatre aspires to raise the consciousness of its audience, as well as its participants. This can be challenging, given the expectations of an audience accustomed to mainstream theatre. Like any marginalised group that has been deprived of the opportunity for self-definition, the actors with disabilities at

InsideOut have discovered that efforts to accommodate mainstream demands can sometimes compromise our authenticity. We cannot try to be something we are not. We are Disability Theatre. Herein lies our true power.

The advocacy mandate of Disability Theatre, evident in its very presence, connects to an educational role. Our educational process is threefold. Initially, we educate actors with disabilities to realise their own artistic potential. Next, we educate the general public about issues relating to disability. The final aspect of our educational activity arises from collaboration. At InsideOut Theatre, we have discovered the truth of Erving Goffman's observation that not only do we need to educate theatre and society, but we also need to promote a level of comfort before a healthy relationship can flourish.

The general public tends to be afraid of disability. As a result, people with disabilities are compelled to promote a comfort level for people without disabilities. At least sufficient comfort required, to give us the assistance we sometimes need in order to be as independent as possible. For example, a blind person must solicit help to read a menu that is not in Braille or large print. A person in a wheel chair must ask for assistance with a heavy, difficult-to-open door that, unbelievably, is the door to a wheelchair accessible bathroom. Asking for occasional help is a balancing act. Getting the help we need while we strive to maintain our own independence is an art form, it requires great practice, patience, and often, good acting abilities.

Traditionally, individuals with disabilities who were unable to live independently were subjected to the dehumanising impact of institutions. The de-institutionalisation process has, over the past fifty years, seen a variety of shifting trends in rehabilitation. One theory suggests that people with disabilities be placed in completely mainstream settings, and this creates a paradox to my mind. Specifically, if it is not acceptable for individuals with disabilities to assemble with other individuals with disabilities, then what is implied about having a disability? At InsideOut Theatre, nothing is more satisfying than having an entire cast of adults with complex disabilities complete a scene, several scenes, or an entire show successfully without the aid of a single facilitator. That is exciting—much more exciting than watching an individual with a disability acting a token role in a mainstream production, and certainly much more exciting than watching an actor without a disability assuming the role of an individual with a disability. This does not detract from the acting skill required to successfully play the part of a person with a disability: it is simply that acting skill and advocacy in this case are separate considerations. The aim of Disability Theatre is to encompass both.True acceptance of people with disabilities has not occurred with the theatrical community or mainstream audiences; perhaps in part, because facing a disabled actor puts us uncomfortably in touch with our own sense of mortality.[9]

InsideOut Theatre continues to invite theatre companies into partnership. In addition to the inevitable striving towards more and more acceptance and participation on the part of actors with disabilities, collaborative projects produce two additional favourable outcomes. First, the profile of Disability Theatre is raised through the inevitable exposure that occurs when partnering with well-known theatre artists or companies. Second, artists in mainstream theatre gain valuable training and awareness working alongside actors with disabilities. This latter benefit is often surprising to actors who enter the partnership with preconceived notions of the disability culture.

Just as the competitive nature of patriarchy sadly serves an

---

[9] Consider, as Taylor has done, the "confusing effect on the audience" when watching a classic fool in performance. "At one moment we are watching some poor fool make a mess of everything he attempts, and at the next time we look, we find the mirror slanted to reflect our own faces" (p. 83).

entitled few, the elitist nature of traditional theatre promotes the myth that creativity belongs to a talented select. That is, those who are able to earn a living with their craft. How has the InsideOut process challenged this notion and successfully attracted audiences? Not with aggression and opposition, which would create an inevitable backlash, but with authentic, empowering Feminist practices, like teaching and focusing on others.

Once on stage, actors with disabilities are nurtured to attain two goals: autonomy and realisation of their true right to theatrical expression. We then move to wooing the audience with soul connection. The eruption of genuine laughter from the audience speaks for itself, and the frequently heard post-show comment, "It makes me feel like I could be a performer." is evidence of the power of our process and performance. Progress, nevertheless, is slow and steady. Changing the attitudes of the general public has always been arduous, but as the history of Feminism has taught us, true change only occurs in small increments. Disability Theatre is clearly on the right track despite resistance, as Disability Arts festivals flourish globally.

My personal journey, as well as the evolution and flowering of InsideOut Theatre and of Disability Theatre in general, attests to the idea that achieving the impossible is not only a worthy goal, but the best and most rewarding kind of goal. The heart of our message to the public speaks of our desire to challenge convention, to take our rightful place onstage, and tell our own stories.[10]

---

[10] In Taylor's discussion of the European tradition of the Feast of Fools held during midwinter, he states: "Midwinter foolishness seeks to turn everything upside-down...We get transformed into ...what we are not." It was a time for players to comment on "the day-to-day business of life. They staged satirical plays which showed the proud and mighty as foolish." (Pp. 93-94).

Ruth Bieber

CHAPTER THREE

Belonging

The Transition Years

During my years as a counsellor, before the inception of InsideOut Theatre, I used drama games and activities to fortify the therapeutic process in group and individual counselling sessions. Therefore, when it was suggested that I incorporate the element of performance, the group participants were suddenly transformed into actors. The notion of recruitment did not occur to me initially; that came later, as did the unfolding realisation of the transformative power of performance. Two important variables arose from this transformation which ultimately became the criteria for participating in my drama groups.

The first variable: Participant/actor must have a desire to perform. This might seem entirely too obvious, but within social service agencies, there can exist a requirement for a 'referral' in order to receive services. Our members could be referred by a human services practitioner as part of an Individual Program Plan (IPP). In this case, it is important to discern the source of the request for participation. Is it the potential group member, who wishes to experience the dramatic arts? Or, is it a keen referring agency representative; perhaps an enthusiastic parent? Potential participants/actors do not need previous experience in performance but they must have an interest in performing. Herein lies one of the greatest distinctions between Mainstream theatre and the InsideOut process. Where theatre seeks the experienced and best fitting actor, we simply require that the participant /actor possess a desire to risk the exposure that accompanies performance. Within the human services field, 'participant' is often used instead of 'actor' or 'artist'. It took me years to become comfortable with the jargon that typically accompanies the theatre arts. For a pointed example, the very first InsideOut performance took place in a church auditorium in 1993. I certainly had an acting background, but knew little about mounting a performance. Perhaps I did not feel worthy of using words like 'actor', 'rehearsal' and 'company'—normal terms within the theatre arts community. I was more comfortable using words like 'participant', 'session' and 'group'. This did change eventually, coinciding with our acceptance into the theatre arts community.

The second variable: Participant/actor must possess basic group skills. I learned this second guiding principle the hard way. Many individuals wish to perform, but some want to dominate the stage. This is not appropriate for a theatrical cooperative. Time and energy is best devoted to working within the collective. Frequently, the participants/actors with disabilities exhibit a pronounced, survival-type of 'egocentrism'. This occurs naturally as a result of constant medical attention and the necessity of getting daily needs met by others.

In the early days, many individuals who were referred to InsideOut came from large group homes or institutions. Social skills developed within the dramatic process produced favourable results in community living. Much literature details the benefits of drama, with reference to development of social skills and the increase in self-confidence. This is the case with many InsideOut participants who start as social isolates and become community participants. A basic foundation of social consciousness, however, must exist within them first.

These two fundamental variables have rarely failed me. Regardless, it does take time to assess the actual level of interest and/or social ability for any actor. It became evident that we had to meet differing needs due to varying skill levels.

My previous experience involving people with varying disabilities was extraordinarily useful where diagnostic profiles were concerned, and this was an important point of departure between the rehabilitation community and me. Some rehabilitation theorists are uncomfortable with the idea of 'labelling'. I can appreciate associations with labels such as Down Syndrome or autism. While absent in daily communications, as a facilitator/director, I rely on diagnostic identification for safety planning. Ultimately, awareness and planning for any and all medical emergencies[11] is accepted as a demonstration of respect for the participant/actors, rather than a declaration of their limitations.

It is important to offer a number of entry levels and learning opportunities to potential participant referrals or recruits. I have discovered three levels of theatre arts training are ideal. The skill level and previous experience of each actor dictates which group she or he is eligible to join. Over time, many InsideOut actors involve themselves in more than one theatre group. Additionally, some actors evolve into, or for that matter out of, various training programs. For example, the most basic training group is open to all skill levels of participants/actors. This group consists of the broadest range of members with disabilities and offers exciting and exploratory theatrical possibilities. Facilitators establish rules of conduct at the beginning of each ten or twelve-week session with the knowledge that frequent reminders might be

---

[11] I currently teach a credit course at the University of Calgary, which originally was taught to me by Dr. Bernie Warren, who became the first of my many mentors along the road to becoming the Artistic Director of my own theatre company. The course, "Integrating the Arts in Rehabilitation," should more accurately include the word "society" since any rehabilitation community is only a sub-culture of a larger society. Inherent in this course is a discussion of the contextual relevance of behaviour, which, revolutionary in its day, is now far better understood and accepted. For further information, please see the appendices or contact the author.

necessary. Support partners accompany those actors who require extra attention. Once in session, we expect everyone to participate to the best of her/his ability. InsideOut promotes an integrative process; hence, facilitators, volunteers, and support partners participate fully alongside the actors. Theatre is the great equaliser, and commonly, previously uninterested support partners become acting enthusiasts themselves.

All InsideOut theatre groups are inclusive in nature, but the beginner training sessions tend to offer the lowest ratio of integration. Group facilitators must necessarily possess a fine balance of expertise for both drama training and for working with specialised populations. Professionals who wish to facilitate with InsideOut Theatre often possess a stronger leaning towards one or the other discipline. With mentoring, they evolve to incorporate strengths from both disciplines into their practice.

Many actors require no support: relishing their independence. Very few have ever been asked to leave the basic training group. As an example, a young man who managed to start a fire in the washroom while unattended was not dismissed from the group but instead invited to return with supervision. Some members of the company enjoy the benefits of the touring and/ or scriptwriting groups but later return to the basic training program after tiring of the rigours and high level of commitment involved in travel and public performance.

Originally, not all training levels included the opportunity to perform before an audience, either specially invited or the general public. Engaging in drama games and activities within the context of the group itself with other group participants acting as audience members was sufficient. Gradually, however, it became clear that a final performance culminating at the group's end was both desired and ideal.

In 1993, InsideOut Theatre proudly presented its first performance as a service option for a local rehabilitation agency. This was our relatively quiet beginning, and for several years afterwards, the trend continued in a church auditorium with a single group giving one yearly performance. The theatre arts community was slow to recognise this exciting phenomenon as valid artistic expression. Yet, the rehabilitation community was quick to respond and hungered for more. The enthusiasm expressed by people with disabilities, their assistants, and rehabilitation practitioners sparked the creation of two alternate drama-training programs: 'Storytelling' and 'Drama for Transition'. Neither of these programs culminated in final performances. For years, these non-performance training programs flourished until an evolutionary shift occurred, and the artists expressed their desire for a final performance. At that time, InsideOut was the only Disability performance company in the province of Alberta.[12]

'Storytelling' evolved into 'The Scriptwriting Group'. 'Drama for Transition' also evolved, becoming 'A Second Look at InsideOut' (now known as 'A Second Look'). In both cases, members were actor /participants not otherwise engaged during weekdays but wanting to perform, while avoiding the rigors of touring and public performance. With the inception of 'The Scriptwriting Group' and 'A Second Look', the original InsideOut group became 'The Touring Group'.

Ultimately, the story of InsideOut is a story of flexibility and openness. Quite literally, as a theatre company, InsideOut evolved and flourished by responding to the needs and desires of its actors, as well as to theoretical and ideological trends within the rehabilitation community. In the mid-

---

[12] It is important to note here that some rehabilitation theorists tended to focus on the specialized nature of InsideOut rather than the consciousness-raising of disability through the medium of theatre.

nineties, the company incorporated and obtained charitable status, an important move towards financial viability. As a separate entity, InsideOut Theatre began to consume the lion's share of my time and energy. Thus, in the year 2000, I left the counselling profession and, in order to stay true to my vision, took on the theatre company full-time. This decision was truly a leap of faith, one that brought me great rewards and challenges.

Mentoring the Support Workers and Facilitators

Practitioners who work with unique populations in Disability Theatre tend to come from one of two streams; the theatre arts or human services. It is a rare but welcome surprise to find a facilitator/director who possesses previous experience in both domains. Given the tendency of the theatre community to hold fast to its traditional idea of production, early suspicion of InsideOut was evident. I learned quickly the importance of mastering jargon. Terms like 'blocking' or 'a special' were useful when developing technical supports or production strategies. Upon reflection, I find it ironic that theatre artists are typically thought of as adventuresome, whereas, human services practitioners are viewed as conservative. My experience has been the reverse. It is the professionals from the human services fields who painstakingly shift, define, and redefine the process to be respectful and inclusive. Professionals drawn to InsideOut Theatre, regardless of their prior orientation, possess an equal passion for creative expression with an instinct for its inherent benefits. The InsideOut process itself focuses on the strengths and attributes of all its members, and we welcome all perspectives as opportunities for learning and growth.

Support partners are care-givers unique to the field of rehabilitation and social work. Their job is to support an adult with disabilities in the community. If their client is referred to the InsideOut program, they facilitate attendance and integration. Some practitioners, but not all, hold diplomas in social work or rehabilitation. Support practitioners are not paid by InsideOut Theatre as the facilitator and directors are; rather, they receive remuneration from a supervising service agency connected to the actor with a disability. As noted, these practitioners have twin roles; supporting their client, while participating in the theatrical process themselves. A favourite InsideOut saying is, "There are no spectators, only participants."

Production proceeds slowly when working with actors who have complex disabilities. Good timing and effective rhythm are critical elements in theatre production, and the participation of support workers is valued to this end. The emotional safety of the InsideOut process is evidenced in my favourite story of the shy support worker who eventually chose to appear onstage playing a lovely guitar solo. While InsideOut performers are encouraged to accept the risks inherent in any performance, they know they are not expected to go beyond the limits of their comfort zone. Actors eventually find their boundaries - the edges of which shift and change over time.

The blurring of roles in the InsideOut process also promotes safety. Unlike traditional theatre, which makes clear distinctions between members and their differing roles, InsideOut actors enjoy equality. I never expect a company member to do something that I am not prepared to do myself. InsideOut actors learn they will not be embarrassed or abandoned onstage. Confidence grows, and we reinforce the InsideOut philosophy by beginning and ending each performance with "Together we're? ... InsideOut!!"

The on-going success and evolution of any small theatre company lies in the dedication and passion of those who do not fear to swim upstream. Professionals, volunteers, protégés, attendants, and actors demonstrate courage, creativity, and commitment to this important work, because it offers immeasurable opportunities and many exciting challenges.

Accessibility and Safety

The term 'accessibility' is often applied to physical accessibility exclusively; whereas, in fact, 'accessibility' properly refers to a broad range of tenets. A more accurate term might be 'access-ability' in reference to physical and emotional accessibility as well as safety in communication and interpersonal relationships. Addressing each accessibility issue is paramount to the InsideOut rehearsal process, in order to maintain safety at all levels of the human experience. This is the heart of the InsideOut message to the community at large. Facilitators and program coordinators are responsible for accommodating the safety needs of each group member. This harkens back to the List of Guiding Principles at InsideOut.

A therapy group can take place in almost any comfortable room. A theatre arts collective requires adequate acoustics, a large suitable space, together with appropriate accessibility. These were the important issues in the mid-1990s, before the company began performing in theatrical venues. A centrally located church auditorium with wheelchair accessibility, an outdoor entrance, and easy access to washrooms provided a suitable stage, as well as a low-cost rehearsal hall.[13]

Regularly scheduled rehearsal times are also important since many actors rely on public transit. For these reasons, InsideOut offers weekly rehearsal sessions which are ninety minutes to two hours in length. This not only allows for scheduling regularity, but also avoids actor fatigue. People who face the daily challenges imposed by a variety of disabling conditions may tire, or become confused if too much variation is introduced.

---

[13] Many thanks to the Hillhurst United Church in Calgary for its on-going support and dedication to Disability Theatre.

Since facilitators must be prepared to respond to a variety of medical conditions, such as seizures, diabetic comas, adverse drug reactions, and much more, it is imperative to have easy access to a cell phone in case of emergency. At the beginning of each twelve week session, actors complete a registration form, highlighting data and contact information and any specific, relevant issues related to their disabilities. Some actors might take issue with the request for diagnostic details; however, I cannot overemphasize the importance of this information for ensuring safety. Recall the individual with tunnel vision mentioned in chapter one, who was hesitant to divulge his legal blindness, which is ironic, considering my own vision disability.

The very first InsideOut performance chose Integration as its theme. We called the show *Belonging* because this theme depended on the sharing of each person's experiences and feelings. The fact emerged that at many times in their lives, the actors did not feel a sense of belonging. As facilitators, we acknowledged their deeply felt distress, and fostered sensitivity among the group members. We also discovered that the use of humour provided an excellent buffer against emotional overload, as well as great healing opportunities. Years later, we found research that supported the therapeutic benefits of laughter. Actually centuries before, Zen Buddhists' teachings demonstrated "that humour is a many-edged weapon, which can be brandished just for the fun of it, or wielded with consummate skill as an instrument of spiritual surgery."[14] Humour has become the InsideOut trademark. Actors are often heard explaining how uplifted they feel after each rehearsal. In fact, many group members say, "InsideOut is the highlight of my week."

The use of humour also provides an important buffer between artists and audience members. Regular InsideOut audience members look forward to our annual performances with great anticipation. Occasionally, in order to see the

---

[14] Taylor, p. 7.

humour in the serious message, they have to laugh at themselves. Over the years, we may have lost some audience members who figuratively saw themselves onstage, but could not appreciate the humour. Marginalised populations offer shocking stories which could involve any one of us, meaning anyone could be a possible target.

With InsideOut, we learn to laugh at one another, at our audience, and, best of all, at ourselves. As the art critic James Elkins reflects, "There is ultimately no such thing as an observer or an object, only a foggy ground between the two." Elkins goes on to explain that the observer evaporates, and instead a "betweenness" occurs, where part of us is the object, and part of the object is us."[15]

Inherent in our process is a belief in the unalienable right to express our thoughts and feelings without censorship, unless these thoughts and feelings break the ground rules against bullying and general disrespect. Over the years, InsideOut Theatre has enabled communication with the help of sign language interpreters, picture communicators (Bliss Boards), Braille, audio cassette tapes, and communication software. We include and communicate with individuals who are nonverbal. Our aim is to accommodate the needs of every actor, regardless of skill level. Virtually any individual's unique qualities can ultimately become a performance opportunity. Recall the actor, mentioned earlier, who almost without fail answered every question by saying, "Yes." It was our job as facilitators to organise his parts by incorporating this ability into the performance.

A number of ethical dilemmas arise when we merge artists with disabilities with the theatre arts community, due in part to its code of ethics or near lack thereof. I have often thought that comparing these ethical differences is a useful exercise. Fundamentally, ethics of all disciplines depend on

---

[15] *The Object Stares Back: On the Nature of Seeing*, p. 44.

weighing the benefits and risks for the individual against the benefits for the larger population. As a counsellor, I had always understood the importance of ethical awareness, in spite of professional variations. I was surprised, therefore, to learn that the theatre arts possess no overt documented code of ethical conduct. For this reason, it was on rare occasion, more challenging to incorporate theatre-trained artists into the InsideOut rehearsal process than practitioners from the human services field. I recall one incident when an impatient actor/facilitator with years of theatre experience physically pushed an actor with a disability for moving slowly. The action caused the disabled actor to fall to the floor. Like many InsideOut artists, the actor in question, possessed a mild brain injury that prevented her from processing commands quickly.

'Slow and steady' and 'repetition, repetition, and more repetition' are the fundamental elements of every InsideOut rehearsal. The unique qualities of individual actors must be supported in every way possible. In order to promote creative expression, no one must be humiliated or embarrassed about a condition over which he has very little, if any, control.

It is vital that no individual actor be permitted to dictate entire sessions with consistent behavioural mismanagement or dominate with egocentrism. Behavioural mismanagement, in my experience, is less of an issue than egocentrism. Social skill development, after all, is one of the many benefits of joining an InsideOut program. Over time, many individuals mature and grow as interpersonal communicators. If, however, the pronounced self-focus of people with disabilities comes with an egocentric desire for admiration, a challenge emerges. "This is not a one-actor performance," is a statement frequently made by InsideOut facilitators.

The ethical considerations around confidentiality can also pose some interesting dilemmas. Actors are assured that no personal stories will be shared beyond the rehearsal without their consent. I recall designing a vignette around a guardianship issue dear to the hearts of many of our adult actors. The show that year was called *Advocacy in Action,* and the vignette was one that I was eager to share with the public. At the last minute, however, the actor in question decided she was not ready to share her story with the world. Sadly, we removed the vignette from the performance, and it remains unperformed. In the end, this was not a total loss, since the therapeutic benefit of sharing common stories while developing the vignette was of tremendous value to all the actors.

A final note regarding interpersonal safety as it relates directly to the first InsideOut script, *Belonging.* The theme of integration, on the surface, is one which relates most directly to people with disabilities; at least, that's what we all thought. Over the production of the inaugural performance, an interesting phenomenon emerged. Not a single vignette within that production related directly to disability. Rather, the issues that emerged from the theme of belonging were, universal, coming from the hearts and previous life experiences of the actors, with or without disabilities. Themes included: 'pressure to consume alcohol at a party,' 'pressure to conform', and 'challenges faced by persons who are ethnically different or live an alternative lifestyle'. The power of theatre to promote dialogue, understanding, and connection was unmistakable and has become the most long-standing trademark of this small, cutting edge theatre company. Are we not all still reaching for our dreams? And do we not all hope to be loved and accepted as we are? Quality of life research, undertaken by Dr. Roy Brown, confirms that we all want the same things from this process we call life: acceptance, meaningful relationships, and a sense of personal value. We all just want to belong.

BELONGING

Tableau

BELONGING

Together

Friendship

Sharing

Drama

Squeeze

Embracing

Victory

BELONG

Vignette 1

A group of people wearing red shirts is in a huddle having a wonderful time and talking loudly. They continually exclude a person wearing a green shirt, who keeps trying to join the party. At this point, the person in the green shirt breaks into an operatic song about rejection.

Vignette 2

Person 1 in red shirt is sitting at a desk.

Person 2 in a green shirt comes in and tries to engage the first person in conversation about last night's party.

Person 1 rejects all these advances at friendship.

Enter Person 3, also in a red shirt, who begins a conversation with Person 1, who immediately and enthusiastically joins in.

Enter Person 4 and 5, both in red shirts, who are immediately accepted into the conversation.

Person 2, in the green shirt, continues to be ignored.

Vignette 3

A large party is happening. Everyone is wearing a red shirt and drinking beer. A green shirt appears at the door and is welcomed in and offered a beer. When he declines the beer, all the others reject him. They all continue to party, but physically exclude him.

Vignette 4

A man wearing a red shirt is preparing to introduce his girlfriend, who is wearing a green shirt, to the family. He is prepping her by telling her who everyone is and what to say. When he introduces his girlfriend to his aunt, the aunt says, "Nice weather." The girlfriend replies, "If you're a duck." The joke falls flat. When he goes to introduce his girlfriend to his uncle, the uncle says, "Nice weather," to which the boyfriend answers, "If you're a duck." Everyone responds with enthusiastic humour.

Vignette 5: Mask Scene

A man in a red shirt comes out and puts on a mask. He is immediately transformed into a happy and enthusiastic character. Enter next man in a red shirt. He dons a mask and is also transformed into a happy character. The same pattern happens with two more characters in red shirts. All the characters are excited and positive. They try to give a mask to a person in a green shirt who repeatedly rejects the mask. This makes all the red-shirt characters feel self-conscious, so they take off their masks and lose all their enthusiasm.

Vignette 6: Father/Son

A man enters the room and explains to his son that he cannot come home for Christmas and is worried that his son will be very disappointed. On the contrary, the son is happy for him and wishes him well over Christmas, and they promise to telephone each other.

Vignette 7

A group of red-shirted people is partying. The person in a green shirt tries to join the festivities and is physically rejected again and again. The green-shirted person initiates a song and gets the audience singing a tune about friendship.

THE END

Ruth Bieber

CHAPTER FOUR

Work, Work, Work

Creative Approaches to Financial Challenges

The late 1990s confronted InsideOut Theatre with two conflicting realities; the company was steadily growing while shackled to a climate of shrinking resources. Potential financial supporters often asked, "You run an entire company on that annual budget?? How do you do it?" Certainly, a home office, a highly subsidised rehearsal space at the local church, and contracted facilitators were vital to the company's fiscal management. There was much more to our financial survival. Fortunately, creativity lends itself to flexibility and problem solving, both on and offstage.

Volunteers play a valuable role in the development of InsideOut Theatre. They fundraise, sit on the Board of Directors, and assist in many facets of production. In Canada, the advent of casino dollars, while controversial, opened many doors for small non-profit organisations like InsideOut.

To qualify for casino revenues, InsideOut registered for non-profit status and elected a voluntary Board of Directors. Board members volunteered in the casinos, recruited other volunteers, and organised fund-raising events like the successful volunteer-powered InsideOut dinner theatre in 2001. InsideOut also benefited from years of volunteer service from people who designed and printed our promotional material. We were also grateful for the work of the volunteer enthusiasts from the realm of human services who performed with us, even though they had no experience in the theatre arts.

The company's on-going connection to the Rehabilitation Studies Programme at the University of Calgary has brought with it the invaluable contribution of practicum students. In exchange for a practical learning experience and a university credit, students have provided the company with youthful enthusiasm, energy, and general support where needed. During a practicum, the company gratefully receives student assistance for record keeping, acting, stage management, technical sound and lighting support, as well as general production including facilitation. Each of these duties is valued in its own right but invaluable with respect to potential program audits.

One of the earliest and largest grants obtained by InsideOut Theatre was completed with the help of a practicum student. In the early 1990s a well-written proposal often ensured a partially, if not fully, funded project. Over time, however, grant dollars became more elusive, and InsideOut Theatre ultimately found itself enmeshed in a rather curious double bind. Initially, the company could receive arts funding because the work was in the area of theatre: It could also obtain funding from human services based on the target population - actors with disabilities. The fiscal glory days were short lived, however, and the dual funding ultimately backfired. Arts funders began to point the company in the direction of human service funding agencies and vice versa, leaving the company financially compromised. In the end, InsideOut successfully established that both mandates were being met and received funding based on its dual commitment to provide theatre training and performing opportunities to participant/actors with disabilities.

The categorical dilemma was only the beginning, as two new challenges arose. There was an increase in the number of grant applications from other similar non-profit groups, coupled with a decrease in the number of granting organizations. In the late 1990s, InsideOut Theatre lost human resource dollars from three levels of government, as programs were eliminated. The funds were replaced largely by lottery and gambling revenues. [16]   Other fiscal opportunities came from non-credit adult learning, and private and corporate donors.

Although funding for arts programs is still available, it has seen little growth within a conservative political climate. This is particularly true for smaller independent companies like InsideOut Theatre.   In 2000, at a forum in Calgary, an international expert in municipal arts explained that the average dispensation of civic dollars to the Arts was four percent.   Calgary, however, was spending less than one percent, and most of these dollars supported a single annual event.   A subsequent provincial study clearly showed the fiscal benefits of the Arts to any municipality.   Despite this data small theatre companies do not receive the financial support enjoyed by sports organizations or larger, professional theatre companies.

A further challenge exists for InsideOut Theatre in that we do not offer a 'regular season' of productions.   Rather, we enjoy the flexibility that comes with open invitations from interest groups who wish to be educated and entertained.   InsideOut Theatre has performed by invitation at numerous conferences, volunteer appreciation evenings and other events.   Special invitation performances rarely contribute financially to the operating costs of the company.   A nominal performance fee is charged, while the greatest benefits of invited shows result in; promotion, education, and advocacy. Registration fees and membership dues are intentionally nominal in accordance with the company's accessibility obligation.   The majority of our actors are financially marginalised. They enjoy benefits of the dramatic arts with InsideOut Theatre at a highly subsidised rate.   The acquisition of sufficient operating dollars requires dedication and focus from the Artistic Director or General Manager.

---

[16] In Alberta's Conservative political climate, organisations must run these casinos, a process that requires tremendous time and energy.

Core funding and project funding differ. Core funding, otherwise referred to as operating dollars, supports the infrastructure of an organisation, while project funding is allocated to a specific project. Operating costs include capital expenditures, salaries, and general overhead. One distinction between community and professional theatre is in the allocation of operating dollars. Community theatres rely heavily on volunteers and project funding, whereas professional theatres often receive financial support for their day-to-day operations from all three levels of government. Professional theatre companies can also receive funding for a specific project but this allocation is separate from regular operations. Community theatres rarely receive sufficient operating funds and this strains administration and promotion. A community theatre may apply for project funding, but this inherently results in a Catch-22.

Proposal writing requires time and energy. Community theatre artists are usually volunteers with day jobs, working to pay their own household bills and volunteering their time towards the production. Who is left to write proposals? Although InsideOut Theatre is not a community theatre, it has experienced this dilemma. In 2000, I resigned from my counselling therapy position to become the full-time Artistic Director of InsideOut Theatre. The goal, to obtain core funding, had previously not been necessary. As the sole bread winner at home, I needed a salary. Initially, it was an on-going financial struggle. Miraculously, the household bills got paid and InsideOut continued to thrive. During this timeframe, the company hired an assistant.

With the advent of this second position, InsideOut experienced the 'proposal writing run-around'. Like me, the new staff person wore several hats with administrative duties a low priority. The position should have been half-time, but the company forged ahead in an attempt to financially support a second full-time staff. Researching and preparing proposals to fund this new position grew to be a major part of the job description. After two years it became apparent the cycle was counter-productive. We eventually realized full-time proposal writing was required in order to generate dollars for the position itself. Funds potentially available for programme expansion were compromised. Out of desperation, InsideOut Theatre turned to a professional fund-raiser.

Trained fund-raisers are expensive but they will often defer salary until funds have been secured. I have always said that InsideOut's best promotion is its shows. The company's first professional fund-raiser had seen our show and was enthusiastically convinced of her ability to raise funds for this small theatre initiative.

She soon learned about the myth of corporate charity. Large corporations do donate millions to charity, but these funds are often inequitably distributed. Each corporation supports a favourite charity, and adult actors with disabilities requiring guardianship support do not seem to attract corporate and private donors.

Another strategy used by InsideOut Theatre for successful fiscal management is the sharing of resources via 'partnership'. The company has struck partnerships with a variety of theatre arts organisations and community rehabilitation groups. These arrangements have been an effective source of mutual support, particularly when resources are complementary. InsideOut employs freelance theatre artists, resulting in skill development and promotional opportunities for the company. In return, financially struggling local performers receive part-time work and gain experience by working with actors with disabilities. In keeping with our Feminist approach, the collaborative partnerships have always been the most fruitful for the company as a whole. This has been true for productions, workshops, and new initiatives.

Funding grant requirements often have parameters that may

or may not mesh with company goals and aspirations. Project grant applicants are required to meet specific criteria prior to applying. A number of these criteria include: a Board of Directors, a working Governance board, a strategic plan and proof of long term sustainability. This final criterion can lead to an inescapable vortex for two reasons. First, paradoxically, the successful acquisition of a project grant often leads to staff fatigue because now the company needs the people power required to complete its new initiative. If the company possesses few or no operating funds, staff are pulled from regular administrative duties to complete the new project. Second, with the strain placed on existing resources, there is the ultimate question of future sustainability. The key to this dilemma is in applying for funding that meshes as closely as possible with the goals and philosophy of the theatre company, rather than obtaining funds for funds' sake.

The following script highlights one of InsideOut Theatre's most creative approaches to the project grant conundrum. The company had successfully obtained a sizable provincial grant with the proviso the project in question have an employment focus. Many InsideOut actors attend our programs as a means of alleviating work-related stress. Their faces dropped when I announced the theme of that season's production had to be about employment. In response to their lamentations, the following compromise was struck. The production would come in two parts. The first would explore employment-related challenges and solutions for people with disabilities. The second part would focus on employment fantasies. Ultimately, the production resulted in a tremendously enjoyable, therapeutic, and educational experience. It wasn't just about 'work, work, work'.

WORK, WORK, WORK

Tableau

Person 1: (*steps forward*)   Work.

Person 2: (*steps forward*)   Express.

Person 3: (*steps forward*)   Customer Relations.

Person 4: (*steps forward*)   Hard.

Person 5: (*steps forward*)   Boring.

All together: Work.

Tableau

Person 1: (*steps forward*)   Fantasy work.

Person 2: (*steps forward*)   Fulfilment.

Person 3: (*steps forward*)   Rewarding.

Person 4: (*steps forward*)   Helping others.

Person 5: (*steps forward*)   Respect.

All together: Fantasy work.

They disperse to set first vignette.

Host: (*centre stage*) Good evening, welcome. All of these people have disabilities, and this is our play. The work we do is never done.

Vignette 1

A: (*on phone*) Your order was so large, we don't have it finished… (*Turning to audience*) The supervisor hung up on me. This is so stressful. She gives me this huge order that I cannot complete on time.

Supervisor: (*enters*) The workers should work harder.

A: Come with me. Come on. I think you need to have a seat. You can see the workers are going as quickly as they can. They cannot go any faster.

Supervisor: They have to work harder.

A: If you had listened to me on the telephone, you would have heard one of my solutions. You can take what we have done now and get the rest later.

Supervisor: That would work.

A: And next, if you gave us the order a bit earlier we wouldn't be in this dilemma.

Supervisor: I appreciate your finding a solution. We can call it a day.

Actors leave stage.

Host: (*centre stage*) People often neglect to ask us how we feel about the work we do. (*exits*)

Vignette 2

Counsellor: So, Tannis, glad you came in today. How are you doing?

Tannis: Fine.

Counsellor: So, since I am your employment counsellor, I am assuming that you came in here today to talk about your job search. Is it going OK? So, what do you want?

Tannis: I want a different job. I am getting bored.

Counsellor: So what do you have in mind?

Tannis: I would like to work in a dentist's office.

Counsellor: That is a good idea, but I am not sure you would like it, so I think we should call a conference to discuss it.

Enter many others.

Counsellor: Here they all are. As the chair, we should introduce ourselves.

Psychiatrist: Will this job meet her emotional needs?

Mother: I am here to make sure she gets another job to keep her from hanging about and getting stressed out.

Tannis: Hi.

Dentist: I am a dentist, and I would be her work placement.

Support: I am here to make sure everything decided on today is for her best interests.

Counsellor: Let's begin the discussion with insights about Tannis.

Psychiatrist: Will she receive enough support and a loving environment?

Support: I hope this environment will not be chaotic. She does not need high stress levels.

Dentist: The job is not too easy, and takes a lot of training and years of study. She needs to be on time and committed.

Professionals talk among themselves simultaneously, not listening to each other and ignoring Tannis.

Tannis: (*stands up*) (*to audience*) I like to work alone. (*exits*)

One by one the professionals decide they have to leave.

Psychiatrist: (*looks at watch*) Oh, I have my next patient in ten minutes.

Each of the others also excuses themselves until finally the employment counsellor is alone onstage and only then notices that Tannis, the client, is gone. Counsellor exits stage calling for Tannis.

Host: (*centre stage*) In the next vignette, Helen is trying to do her work while others around her are creating havoc.

Vignette 3

A: Did you lose your pen again?

B: Yes. Have you seen it?

C: I need to talk to you, Helen. There is a crisis. Please, Helen.

A: You always have a crisis. You don't need me. I am working.

B: I want your help now.

A: Not now.

Crowd gathers of people speaking loudly and distracting Helen from her work.

A: Everyone out of my office, please. Excuse me, I am working hard, and you guys are needy and disrespectful. I need to do my job, and you need to do yours.

Crowd: Sorry, Helen.

A: Thanks for listening.

Crowd: Good thing you spoke up. (*Everyone exits.*)

Host: (*centre stage*) Have you ever wanted to scream at someone for making a lot of unnecessary mistakes? Watch the supervisor do that in the next scene.

Vignette 4: Conflict: major frustration and an irate customer

Supervisor: That's not the right X-ray. What have you been doing all morning?

Technician: (*sighs and rubs forehead*) I'm doing my best.

Supervisor: Well, your best isn't good enough! You have had so much training, and you've messed up. You have given me the wrong X-ray.

Technician: I guarantee that I will sort it out. I am on it.

Janitor: (*enters room, with broom*)

Supervisor: When is that going to happen? Christmas is coming, too.

Janitor: Excuse me. He (She) has been working a lot this weekend and has been here today since 6:00 this morning. Maybe he (she) needs a break, and he'll (she'll) be more efficient.

Supervisor: Oh! I didn't realize that. Yes, a break. You should take a break. In fact, maybe *I* need a break. (*to audience*) Nothing is going to get solved by just yelling at the employee. (*to technician and janitor*) OK, let's take a break.

Host: (*centre stage*) Work, work, work. Maybe we all need a break, and after intermission, please come back for the second half of our show, when we look at work the way we want it to be.

Tableau

Fantasy work

Hollywood star

Archaeologist

Writer

Gourmet Chef

Professional

Lawyer

Rock star

Fantasy Work

Vignette 1: Job Fair

A: Alana, how lovely to see you. So welcome to this year's job fair. Is there anything that you're interested in?

B: I don't really know.

A: Well, let me show you what we have here today. We have Michelle. Michelle is a professional, as you can see.

B: Do you have any available jobs?

M: Well, actually, I do have some things that have come out this very week.

B: Do they have any benefits?

M: That's not what this is about.

B: Awww…

A: Well, just tell her about…

M: Well, you get to express yourself, and you have lots of free time. You can work whenever you want, and if you don't like it, then it's OK. We just party.

A: (*interested*) How flexible are the hours?

M: My workers are running me ragged because they never are here, and they never show up on time.

B: Do you have any tax exemptions?

M: I'm not really able to discuss my personal tax information.

A: She's got in trouble before a couple of times.

B: What is that you do exactly?

M: Well, it was nice meeting you.

B: It was nice to meet you too.

A: Well, next we have a very special guest, Stephen King.

B: Cool.

S: Good afternoon.

A: We want you to tell us what it's like to be a writer.

S: It's really a fabulous way of earning a living. I feel so grateful to all of my faithful readers.

B: Yes, I love your stories, and I am actually a member of your fan club! When's your next book coming out?

S: Do I have to write another one? (*to A*) You told me I was here to tell *other* people how to write! (*stomps offstage*)

B: I didn't get his autograph.

A: Next we have a very different job. This is Ben.

B: Nice to meet you.

C: Hi, Ben.

A: He's a bus driver.

C: Yeah. And people make too much noise in the back of the bus.

A: So what do you do when they make too much noise?

C: I tell people to be quiet.

B: Do they listen?

C: No.

A: Do they work you pretty hard?

C: Yeah, but I get to travel a lot, driving the bus, because people like to go to all kinds of places.

A: Do you have anything special to ask, Ben?

B: Nope.

A: OK. Well, then, thank you for your time.

B: It was a pleasure to meet you.

C: Thank you, bye.

A: Last, we have a very important job. Brian is the CEO.

B: Really! A CEO! What is that?

D: It stands for Chief Executive Officer.

B: Wow! Chief Executive Officer of what?

D: Oh, that doesn't matter. The important thing is to know that I'm in charge.

A: Doesn't that mean you have a lot of responsibility and stress?

D: Not if you hire the right people to do the work.

A: So what's your favourite thing about being a CEO?

D: Vacation time – lots of vacation time.

B: That sounds like my kind of job!

A: Well, thank you.

D: My pleasure. (exits)

A: So, I showed you a variety of jobs today, are there any that you would want to do?

B: No doubt about it – vacation is the way to go; I'll be a CEO.

A: Right. Good luck.

Vignette 2: Newspaper

Two people are onstage typing. In comes Jean.

Jean: (*flustered*) Ohhh nooo!!! I am having the worst personal crisis, Ryan, and I see you're already angry with me, but that piece I said I would have ready for the morning paper…it's not done!

Boss: Umm…I've warned you before about this.

Jean: I know you've warned me. You said you'd fire me, but can I have another chance? I'm just so stressed!

Boss: I guess so, but this is the last time.

Jean: Oh, that's great! But what are you going to do about today's paper?

Typist: Excuse me, I couldn't help but overhearing, and I have an article that we could put in.

Boss: Really? Show it to me.

Jean: Oh, do you? Well, that's how I got started.

Vignette 3: A famous person getting interviewed on SCXY - TV.

Four people are onstage: an interviewer, a typist, a movie star, and her agent.

Reporter: Good afternoon, this is SCXY – TV, and I'm Maggie. Today on our show we have Helen, who just finished a starring role in a new movie, and she's going to be talking about it. Good afternoon, Helen. How are you today?

Helen: I'm fine.

R: And what have you got to tell us about the new movie you made?

H: It's extreme.

R: And who else is starring in it beside yourself?

H: Tom Hanks and Brad Pitt.

R: Really? You know, I heard through the Hollywood grapevine that you and Tom Hanks had a thing, is that true?

Agent: Oh, no, no, no! No personal questions! (*to the typist*) Don't write that down!

R: Next question then; what else happens in the movie?

H: Well, Tom Hanks and I get...

A: I said no personal information. (*to star*) I'm here to protect you.

R: How was it working with Brad Pitt?

H: Yeah, it was really good, he is cute.

R: What a man! Would you like to see him for a date?

A: No, no, no, no! No personal questions!

R: Well, what else can you tell us about the movie then, Helen?

H: Well, it's got a lot of action. Tom and Brad and I...

A: Oh, no, no, no, no!!! No personal questions!!!

R: OK. So tell me about your being pregnant with …

A: No personal questions!!!

R: Well, maybe we should take a break right now. We'll be right back.

Helen and agent go off to the side. They talk.

H: Listen, you can't tell me what to say and what not to say.

A: I'm just trying to protect you.

H: I know, but it's time for the world to know the truth.

A: OK, it's your career. (*They return to the interview.*)

R: And we're back talking with Helen about her new hit movie where she co-stars with Tom Hanks and Brad Pitt. What else do you have to tell us about?

H: I'm engaged to Tom Hanks.

R: Well, folks, you heard it here first. And when is the happy day?

H: Pretty soon.

R: So, do you think Tom and you will get together and make a happy family after this?

H: I think so. I'm already pregnant.

R: Well, folks, stay tuned for the next chapter in Helen's life…could we get an exclusive on that?

H: Sure.

R: Great! Tune in tomorrow, folks, because we will have more exciting stars to interview, and maybe we'll get more dirt.

Vignette 4

Drumheller, an excavation dig for dinosaurs. Three people enter, talking.

Archaeologist 1:   I can't believe I'm here for such an important dig! Oh, this is the find of the century!!!

They all kneel down by the dig.

Archaeologist 2:   Thank you so much for letting me come along on this dig, Dr. Ryan.

Dr. Ryan: That's OK.

A2:   This is so exciting! (*Dr. Ryan is digging.*) Are you onto something Dr. Ryan?

Dr.:   I think so; I found the head of the Tyrannosaurus raptor.

A2:   Oh, is that rare?

Dr.:   Yeah.

A2:   Is it worth a lot of money?

Dr.:   Yeah, it's priceless.

A2:   I can see it there.

A1:   I'm getting so emotional!

A2:   Do you think we should inform someone? This is a major find!

A1:   We should tell the entire scientific community!

Dr.:   Yeah, you're right.

A2:   Well, you two should go do that. I won't keep you. Thanks for letting me come! I'll keep digging.

Dr. Ryan and A1 leave stage left. A2 slowly moves to stage right (SR), where she is greeted by what looks like a thief in a mask.

Thief: So what do you want?

A2:   I heard you're the best thief in the business.

T: That's true. What do you want?

A2:   I need your help.

T: With what?

A2:   A rare dinosaur was found in the sand today, and there is a possibility to make half a million dollars from it.

T: Half a million? I need at least a million before I bother to steal something!

A2:   I only have a half a million on me right now…

T: Then you're wasting my time.

A2:   Half a million now, and three-quarters of a million later, in cash when we're done.

T: OK.

A2:   Here. (*gives money*)

T: OK, I'll meet you back here at exactly midnight, and you tell me where it is.

A2:   It's exactly 100 yards up there in the sand, where the scientists were digging.

T: OK.

A2:   And I don't want any problems.

T: Problems? There'll be no problems.

A2:   Good, I'll see you at midnight then.

T: Goodbye…

A2 leaves the scene, while the thief pretends to leave, then doubles back onto the stage. The thief bends down, takes the dinosaur bones, and then stashes them somewhere else, and runs off. At this time, Dr. Ryan and A1 re-enter the scene.

A1:   Oh, I can't wait for everyone to see this! This is so amazing! (*sees the dig site*) Oh no! The … it's gone! What will the scientific community say? I know…this is a job for…

(*Dr. Ryan and A1 chant*) ... Bone masters!

Everyone chants with the music music.

An officer with a hat and a magnifying glass enters the scene.

BM: I'll find your bones.

A1:   Ohhh...thank you!

The bone master follows a trail across the stage, looking through a magnifying glass, followed by Dr. Ryan and A1.

BM: I have found your dinosaur!

A1:   I'm so happy!

The bone master pulls out the bag of bones.

A1:   Oh thank you...I'm so happy!

A1, the detective, and Dr. Ryan leave the stage. Enter A2.

A2:   Where is that thief? It's almost midnight!

T: Too easy.

A2:   So the job's done?

T: Yeah, I want to see the money.

A2:   I want to see the bones first!

T: I want to see the money!

A2:   Here…see it!

R: It was a piece of cake. Here… (*goes to the stashed bag*) WHAT!!! Where is it!

A2:   Where are the bones? Give my money back!

A2 chases the thief offstage.

THE END

CHAPTER FIVE

School Days

From Institution to Community Inclusion

In 1989, a request came from the University of Calgary that ultimately changed the course of my professional career. The Behaviour Support Team (BST) from the Graduate Rehabilitation Studies Programme was seeking Masters Candidates to apply for a part-time clinical assistantship. The timing was perfect for me to join this team. I had just resigned from a full-time counselling position and, apart from completing graduate studies and raising my first-born son, I did not know what the future held. Eagerly, I seized the opportunity to work and create in this rich and fertile environment, which provided the foundation for InsideOut Theatre.

Although housed at the University of Calgary, the BST was a community service that arose from the deinstitutionalisation movement. Individuals, some who had lived their entire lives in an institution, were referred to the team for support and assistance in making the adjustment to community living. Twenty years later, Calgary could lay claim to hosting dozens of agencies with a similar mandate, but at the time, the BST was cutting edge. This was particularly true, due to the nature of the population served.

The referred clients had unique challenges, often behavioural in nature, which made community living difficult. But this rich academic environment coupled with the truly human-centred philosophy of the team provided an ideal atmosphere for working with special populations and their families.

The team approach was a new and welcome experience in my professional world. Previously, I had been the sole counsellor for children and families at the Canadian National Institute for the Blind in Southern Alberta. I had been quite comfortable working independently but soon learned to appreciate the interdisciplinary power and support of a team approach. The seven years spent with the Rehabilitation Studies Programme, firmly cemented convictions regarding equality; highlighting both rights and responsibilities.

The completion of my graduate work in Theatre and Disability linked significantly to clinical and team duties. With the interdisciplinary nature of community rehabilitation, and the support of Dr. Bernie Warren, a professor in the Drama Department at the University of Calgary, I was able to design a specialized graduate program. While the BST was providing on-going education regarding the importance of community living, my academic studies were focusing heavily on the right to be creative. Clinicians with the team were required to run support groups of a therapeutic nature. My groups always involved drama games and activities, but initially did not culminate in a final performance. This stood in contrast to graduate research findings in performance theory. The inherent benefits of theatrical stage productions for people with disabilities were consistently appearing in the research, steering me closer to the power of performance. In fact, this became the subject of my Master of Education comprehensive examination.

In the early 1990s Richard Campbell, a popular theatre artist from Toronto, joined the BST. Not surprisingly, he co-facilitated with me in the drama groups. Before long, Richard suggested the group on campus shift into the community. This is when the possibility of performance became a reality. Even though I knew little about staging a performance, I was fortified by my passionate theoretical conviction. Other team members focused on more conventional aspects of community living such as employment, educational opportunities, self-care management, and residential needs. In tandem, I was turning toward the right to be creative and, more so, the right to be visible onstage.

Behaviour Support Team members and the rehabilitation community in general were enthusiastically supportive of my endeavours and were often in the audience. Although InsideOut Theatre traces its beginnings to the Rehabilitation Studies Programme, many talented and compassionate artists from the community have supported this burgeoning theatrical creation. The very first InsideOut production was exceptionally fortified in this respect. Richard and I worked with an instructor from the University Drama Department, a professional writer, a singer, and two videographers. The videographers not only taped the performance but also produced the company's first promotional video.

The inaugural performance was a mere ten minutes in length and ultimately became a template for future InsideOut productions. The group explored the theme of 'Integration' using a combination of theatrical modalities including: forum theatre, collective creation, and improvisation. This combination worked well for the actors with disabilities who were still clients of the BST.

Approximately half the cast and crew had intellectual, emotional, and/or behavioural challenges. The remaining actors were community theatre artists. As the clients gained drama skills, the community artists gained knowledge of disability culture. This ultimately built the bridge that was the foundation of what is now known as Disability Theatre, as practised at InsideOut.

Aspects of that successful first show include a collective approach to theme exploration, equal opportunity to perform in a supportive environment, and the videotaping of final performances. Basic performance elements remained with the production for several years until the Touring Group evolved by adding new developments such as backdrops and sophisticated theatrical effects. The trademark of humour endured throughout.

As mentioned, the theme of our first performance was integration, and the show was titled, *Belonging*. The decision to name the first InsideOut performance, *Belonging* arose from the intersection of the Plain Language movement and Feminist philosophy. The Plain Language movement was opportune, as it acknowledged the right of people with intellectual disabilities to understand written material. It promoted full participation through clear and understandable communication with an emphasis on written documentation. The primary focus was on jargon-free speech and uncomplicated wording. Accessible communication became the key for both the rehearsal process and the actual staged performance. There are also parallels between the Plain Language movement and the Feminist insistence on replacing the generic 'he' with gender-specific pronouns.

Both movements embrace maximum participation, thus, give voice to an 'invisible' minority. Moreover, the disability community espoused the tenet of 'People First'. Here, the respectful attitude toward the disability community was fostered by focusing primarily on the human experience and secondarily on the disability. The literature to date has come full circle regarding 'People First'. To promote clarity and acceptance, terms such as 'Deaf actor' rather than 'actor with a hearing impairment' are acceptable, especially in the disability arts community. Being disabled no longer necessitates sitting at the back of the bus. Members of the disability community celebrate contributions while fully participating 'front stage'.

My greatest challenge as a blind Artistic Director occurred in my interactions with a person from the Deaf Community. I clearly recall the young theatre enthusiast who wanted to join InsideOut, regardless of a hearing disability, mild developmental delay, and anxiety disorder. I can remember thinking to myself: "I am blind, and you are deaf. This is impossible." His sheer determination and enthusiasm won me over, and this began my education with the Deaf Community and its politics.

Initially this young man was loath to connect with the Deaf Community because of misunderstandings involving opposing schools of thought which he found confusing. As a result, we had no sign language interpreter, thus communication with him was compromised. After two seasons, I invited a support person who knew sign language to help him. Initially, he was extremely hesitant, but over time, with the tremendous and patient support he received from a number of sources, his trust in the Deaf Community grew. Sign language support was a critical step forward for this actor and proved to be an eye-opening experience for the company.

There were two opposing schools of thought involving Deaf and Hard of Hearing people, particularly with respect to interpreters and sign language service. The two camps of the Deaf Community fell on either side of the integration movement. One camp believed that being Deaf was completely natural, and that people who were not Deaf comprised the marginalised group. This group favoured segregation. The other camp believed there were inherent benefits in community inclusion and assimilation. The two schools of thought spilled into the theatre company due to differing rules of conduct for support practitioners. Certified interpreters for the Deaf were bound by a traditional code of ethics that prevented their participation on stage. Freelance interpreters were not bound by the same regulations, and relished acting opportunities offered while interpreting. The third group, the InsideOut actors who were Deaf just wanted to do theatre. They were not concerned with the politics of the larger Deaf Community. Eventually, InsideOut Theatre added an additional group to its credit: the Sign Theatre project. Members of this initiative possess basic sign language skills, and actors who are Deaf are free to join this segregated program, or remain with one of the alternative integrated groups. The addition of the Sign Theatre project is testimonial to the flexible and accommodating nature of InsideOut Theatre.

A final note regarding sign language interpretation relates to the audience. Prior to this point, the discussion has focused on supports for Deaf actors in rehearsals and onstage. While ethically relevant, providing sign language for audience members can be a complex and costly undertaking. Where possible, InsideOut has always endeavoured to accommodate Deaf audience members.

In addition to sign language interpretation and plain language, InsideOut Theatre uses a variety of strategies to support rehearsals. As the company evolved, the use of sophisticated computer software designed to create music discs emerged to the delight of many actors with disabilities, who were aspiring 'Rock Stars'. The production of music was so popular with the company, that an additional group has been formed called 'Living Voices'. Once again the development of this new project acts as a clear indicator of the company's mandate to support the needs and desires expressed by actor members.

InsideOut facilitator's are responsible for duties, which are two-fold. First is to recognise all unique abilities, particularly in actors with disabilities who have little or no theatre training. Second, to identify and support those who have not yet embraced their right to be onstage. InsideOut facilitators become skilled in spontaneously recognising theatrical potential in every ability, disability, gesture, speech pattern, and so on. As a pointed example, most of the actors in The School Days vignette (at the end of this chapter) had little, if any, theatre background, and half the group had mild to moderate communication challenges. Nevertheless, this particular performance was and is full of rich and varied theatrical expression.

There were two opposing schools of thought in the early 1990s concerning people with disabilities. The Independent Living movement was in full swing in Canada, and the phenomenon of cross-disability emerged with the intent to promote political power through numbers. Alternatively, and soon to follow, the Social Role Valorisation ideology opposed any segregated congregation of people with disabilities, including organisations like InsideOut. The Independent Living movement was much more supportive of the congregation of people with disabilities than was the Social Role Valorisation movement. In my experience, both movements overemphasized theoretical foundations and did not pay sufficient attention to personal choice. In many key respects, the two movements were philosophically juxtaposed. Each made great contributions to disability culture generally, but, both possessed inconsistencies and challenges for client- centered initiatives.

The Independent Living movement frowned on the inclusion of non-disabled support partners (more commonly referred to at the time as attendants). This meant that the non-disabled attendant could not participate in meetings such as therapy groups, planning sessions, or theatre troupes because such situations might be perceived as disempowering for the individual with a disability. As a woman, who is legally blind, I have certainly experienced a sense of disempowerment when people actually speak directly to my sighted guide rather than to me. This can occur even when I am clearly the person in charge or the designated focus of the meeting. Each situation is different, however. A trusted support partner may speak for a person with intellectual difficulties when the person cannot speak for themselves. In this case, it is empowering to have the assistant in attendance.

Inconsistencies in the Independent Living movement were quite evident in Canada by the 1990s. The movement had shifted over time and no longer meshed with the original American Independent Living movement of the 1970s. Two vibrant, powerhouse advocates with disabilities, Ed Roberts and Judith Heumann created the Independent Living movement in the United States. The initial mandate was that people with disabilities were to be independent participants in the community. This did not mean that supports were eliminated. Reasonable accommodations[17] or attendants were kept or put in place because they served independence.

From the perspective of Feminist inclusion, a more serious inconsistency arose from the Independent Living movement, which I termed the 'disability pecking order'. A hierarchical attitude existed in society with respect to disabilities. People with disabilities were tacitly assigned a lesser status. Sadly, this social system was mirrored within disability groups, whereby people with physical disabilities were privileged over those with intellectual challenges. Ultimately, the people with intellectual disabilities were without a voice. Over time a welcome shift occurred within the Canadian movement which is more inclusive of people with intellectual challenges and their support partners. When hierarchy is dismantled, strong, healthy, and empowering bonds develop between individuals who cannot speak for themselves, and their support partners. A final complication; some people from the Deaf Community maintain that they do not possess a disability at all. This vibrant platform of Deaf Culture only serves to add to confusion for groups like InsideOut Theatre.

The convergence of my graduate studies, highlighting the importance of creativity, and my time as a counselor in the Rehabilitation Studies Programme ultimately offered an excellent foundation for what was to become InsideOut Theatre. Graduate and undergraduate students also played

---

[17] Some important accommodations include curb cuts from sidewalk to street, wheelchairs, wheelchair accessible cities and towns, voice activated controls, Braille, kneeling busses, ramps, guide dogs allowed in restaurants and libraries, health insurance, housing, and college scholarships.

invaluable roles in every step of the company's development. The university environment fostered standards of appropriate ethical conduct that reinforced respectful relations among all members of the theatre company. Exposure to relevant research, such as the 'quality of life' work by Dr. Roy Brown, was truly validating. The research supports the notion that the right to participate on the theatrical stage is symbolic of the right to participate on life's stage. More recent research by Dr. Brown provides greater insight into the power of the right brain by highlighting the power of imagery. It is in the feminine brain, the source of creativity and spirituality, that healing occurs, and where miracles are found. Thus, the Rehabilitation Studies Programme was the perfect place for my theatrical education to flourish. Ironically, the theatre community was slow to follow, but in time the gap between theatre and disability narrowed, ultimately creating the new phenomenon of Disability Theatre.

In this chapter I have outlined the impact of changing trends on an independent innovation such as InsideOut Theatre, and more specifically, on the lives of people with disabilities. The shifts in rehabilitation theory influence people with disabilities in ways the larger outside community cannot fathom. The examples given in this chapter are intended to highlight some of these influences and are in no way meant to minimise the profound benefits often resulting from changing theoretical trends. In reality change is stressful, even positive change. InsideOut Theatre and kindred programs are sensitive to this reality, and endeavour to respond to the individual, rather than to a theory or a dictated method of theatre process.

As stated in the concept of 'ableism', the attitude that the non-disabled population is 'superior' results in discrimination against people with disabilities. I have often felt that society would do well to learn from people with disabilities. Having said this, it is important to note that InsideOut Theatre boasts countless successful partnerships with groups and individuals within both the rehabilitation and theatre communities. In the end, we teach each other.

SCHOOL DAYS

Tableau

School days

Yuck

Lots and lots of boys

Hell

Computers

Skipping school

Fun

Skipping ropes

Class pictures

Teacher's pet

Recess

Football

Dances

Desks

Principals

SCHOOL DAYS!!!

Sound cue: school bell

Vignette 1: The Bus

Bus Driver: Another day driving a bus. Those kids drive me totally crazy. Guess I have to pick them up.

Kids: *Bunch of kids acting wild and crazy and loud.*

BD: Sit down, please. Everyone get a seat. I don't want you to throw things out the window. No cursing. No touching things.

Kids: *Acting even wilder. Lots of noise and confusion.*

BD: That is it! I've got the keys, and I quit. You can find your own way to school.

Kids: *Total enthusiasm!*

Kid 1:   That means we have to walk.

Kids: Oh, no. I don't want to walk. What a drag.

They all get off the bus, general complaining.

Sound cue: School bell

Vignette 2: Poetry

Kid 1:   I love this class; it's my favourite.

Kid 2:   It sucks.

Kid 1:   I love the poetry especially.

Teacher: I am your new teacher this semester. We have a new student. Stand up, Ruthie.

Ruthie: Well, I'm not a new student to these guys, just to you. My sister took your class last year.

Teacher: I know, and she was quite terrible. I am sure it runs in the family, and while I'll try to give you a break, I expect you to really apply yourself.

Ruthie: But I am very good at language arts.

Teacher: That's what your sister said, and it was not true. Now, let us begin with poetry.

Ruthie: Yea!

Teacher: Who wants to go first?

Ruthie, madly waving her hand to go first, is ignored by the teacher.

Teacher: Don't go trying to hide from me, class. You, you go first.

Kid 1:   Roses are green, violets are blue, and I don't want to say, and I don't know what to do.

Teacher: Who can do better than that? That deserves a big fat F. You must work harder. You, next.

Kid 2:   *Starts reading a poem (written himself…Everyone is bored and yawning including the teacher. The poem is several pages long.)*

Teacher: Keep on reading, come on.

Teacher falls asleep. Kid 2 continues to read.

Teacher: *(yawning)* You should take that home and read it before bed. Hang on, Ruthie, do you have to go to the bathroom? Sit still, you'll get a chance.

Kid 3: I've been too busy skipping school to write poetry.

Teacher: Big fat F for you. OK. Ruthie get on up. At least try, we don't expect much.

Ruthie: There once was a girl from Peru

Who couldn't tie up her left shoe.

She simply proceeded,

'Til one day she succeeded,

And now she is trying to undo.

Teacher: Very good. Which book did you copy that from?

Ruthie: I didn't get this from a book, I made it up myself.

Teacher: You cannot take credit for other people's work. That is illegal.

Ruthie: I didn't. I did this by myself.

Teacher: Shame on you! That is plagiarism.

Ruthie: I am leaving this school. I am never coming back.

Sound cue: School bell.

Vignette 3: Being Cool

Kid 3:   Hey guys, hi.

Kid 1:   Your teeth are green.

Kid 2:   Is that a hair on your chin?

Kid 3:   Stop that. It hurts.

Kid 1:   Anyways, we are going to have a smoke.

Kid 2:   This is so totally cool.

Kid 3:   Smoking is bad for you. You won't look cool if you are dead. (*exits*)

Kid 1:   I think we look cool.

Kid 2:   What a stupid gym teacher we have.

Enter teacher

Teacher: What is going on? I smell smoke. What are you doing?

Kids: Nothing.

Teacher: You guys are coming to the principal's office right now.

Kid 1:   My mom is going to kill me.

Kid 2:   Guess we should have gone to gym class.

Sound cue: School bell.

Vignette 4: Lunch

Kids: Lunch!!!!!

General chaos and fighting.

Lunch monitor: Stop that right now! Order. Sit down.

No one is paying attention, more chaos and shouting.

Principal: (*enters*) Stop that! You must be quiet or you will get detention.

Students settle down.

Lunch monitor: You guys are wasting the lunch budget.

Principal: Now be good.

Kids: Yes, principal. We'll be good.

Principal leaves. Chaos resumes.

Sound cue: School bell.

Vignette 5: The Exam

Kid 1:   Are you guys ready for this exam?

Kid 2:   I studied all night.

Kid 3:   Did you study everything though? All the chapters?

Kid 2:   Yes, I studied chapter 1.

Kid 3:   You were supposed to study chapters 2 through 12.

Kid 2:   What are you talking about?

Teacher: Sit down, eyes front, get ready for the test.

Kid 2:   Excuse me. This test is on chapter 1, right?

Teacher: No, of course not, it's on chapters 2 through 12. Now get ready.

Kid 2:   The board said chapter 1.

Teacher: Better check your reading. Now is everyone awake? Get with the program. Here are your papers, do not touch your papers until I give the word.

Kid 2:   How much is this test worth?

Teacher: 95% of your grade for the year. Now get ready. One. Two. Three. Go.

Fierce scribbling and writing. Teacher paces and says "get working, no cheating here."

Kid 2 sneaks a look at a book.

Teacher: What are you doing? Give me those books right now. Pick up your pencil and start working.

Teacher: (*compliments other students, randomly saying*) Look at your own paper.

Teacher: Five minutes left.

Kid 2:   What! Five minutes, oh no, I'm dead!

Teacher: Two minutes.

Teacher: One minute.

Teacher: Thirty seconds.

Teacher: 10 ... 9 ... 8 ... 7 ... 6 ... 5 ... 4 ... 3 ... 2 ... 1 STOP. Pencils down, heads up. (*gathers papers up*) These will be marked by 3:00 p.m. today. Next week's test is on chapter 1.

Kid 2:   This is the worst day of my life.

Sound cue: School bell.

Vignette 6: Recess

Kids: Let's play hockey.

Captain 1:   I pick ...

Captain 2:   I pick ...

The two captains divide up the players. One kid is left over.

Captain 1:   You be referee.

Referee: Ready, Go!

Hockey play ensues. Goal is scored.

Referee: One, nothing. Hey, remember this game is for cokes after school.

Hockey play ensues. Goal is scored.

Referee: One, one – a tie.

Captain 2:   Strategy, guys, let's go team.

Hockey play ensues.

Sound cue: School bell rings.

Principal: (*breaking up the game*) All right! Get to class. Go to your classrooms.

Vignette 7: Bullying

Kid 1:   Last class of the day, I'm beat. Hey, buddy, want some gum?

Kid 2:   Yeah.

Kid 1:   (*to Kid 3*) I'd give some to you, but you're too ugly. You're a good sport but...

Teacher: For homework this weekend you have to complete chapters 3, 9, 14, 27, 33... Do I smell gum? Is someone in this room chewing gum?

Kid 2:   Nope, we aren't chewing gum.

Sounds of loud chewing and smacking.

Teacher: Someone here is chewing tangerine gum.

Kid 1:   (*insert a name for X*) is chewing it.

Teacher: Are you chewing gum?

Kid X: No.

Teacher: You might be lying. You look like a liar.

Teacher continues to try to catch the kids.

Kid 1: I'm sure it's *X*. It's probably under her chair.

Teacher: Stand up! (*flips chair*) There it is, the evidence – gum. Off to the principal. (*exits with Kid X*)

Kid 1: What a sucker. We got her again.

Sound cue: bell rings

Kids: School's out. What a day. (*general talking*)

Kid 1: We sure got *X* today. (*They laugh.*)

Kid 2: Look, *Y* is alone. Let's get her/him. Let's make fun of her/him.

Kid 1: Like that shirt, but didn't you wear it every day this week?

Kid 3: You are so ugly, man.

Kid 4: Watch this. Hey *Y*, how is it going? Nice shoes, where did you get them, Kmart?

Kid 5: Hi, *Y*. How are ya doing? Ya know what, you are a disease, and your breath smells just like your butt!

Kid 6: Hi, *Y*. Anyone tell ya how ugly you are?

Kid 7: What's the smell around here? Oh, it's you, *Y*.

Enter Kid X, stays to the side.

Kid 8:   Y, you look a little bit frazzled. Not feeling too good, had a bad day?

Kid 9:   Why are you always alone, Y? No friends?

Kid X: (*aside*) That does it! (*moves up beside Kid Y*) Hey, Y, sorry I'm late. (*talking to the other kids*) If you will excuse us, the teacher is expecting us now.

(*They exit, leaving the bullying kids looking at each other.*)

End scene; cast sings: a heartfelt song about friendship

After School Tableau

Graduation

Chess club

Homework

Basketball

School bullies

Band practice

Milk and cookies

Hockey

Book club

Soccer

Theatre

AFTER SCHOOL!!!

Vignette 8: We are working with the letter…

Kid 2:   What a waste of time.

Teacher: Can you hear me? Where is your hearing aid?

Kid 2:   I forgot it.

Teacher: I have a note for your mother. You must give it to her.

Teacher: Now pay attention. We are working with the letter M. Mmmmmmmm Repeat.

Kid 1:   Mmmmmmmmm

Teacher: Good. Now your turn. Mmmmmmmmm

Kid 2:   Mmmmmmmmm

Teacher: Good.

Teacher: Now say "mother." Mother. Mmmmmmother.

Kid 2:   Mmmmother

Teacher: Good.

Kid 3:   Mother, mother, mother

Teacher: Good. Now you say mother.

Kid 1:   You are not my mother.

Teacher: No back talk, say mother. Now practice more.
MMMMMMM

Class: Mmmmmmmmmmmmmmmmm

Teacher: (*to audience*) mmmmmmmmmmmmmmm

Audience: Mmmmmmmmmmmm

Teacher: I can't hear you. Mmmmmmmmmother.

Audience: Mmmmmother.

Teacher: Good. Good.

Teacher: Now pay attention. Let's practice T.
tttttttttttttttt

Kid 1:   Tttttttttttt

Teacher: Good.

Kid 2:   What?

Teacher: Tttttttttt

Kid 2:   You are stuttering. Tttttttttttttt

Teacher: Good.

Teacher: Say two, two, two, two.

Kid 1:   Two, two two.

Kid 2: Twooooooooooooooooooooooooo.

Teacher: You need to practice more at home.

Teacher: (to audience) T t t t t t t t t t

Audience: T t t t t t t t t t t

Teacher: Louder please and again. Twooooooooo.

Audience: Twoooooooooooo.

Teacher: Now it is time to go home, and come back next week, on time.

Teacher: Now take this note to your mother.

Kid 2:   Right. I'll TTTTTTTTAKE this note home TTOOOOO my Mmmmmother.

Vignette 9: Show and Tell Club

Teacher: Good afternoon, everyone. Welcome to the Show and Tell Club. Now I want to introduce you to the news people from Channel 2 and 7, who have come to videotape our show. Let us show them our best show and tell behaviour.

Kid 1:   We are always good.

Kid 2:   I have brought some pictures of my vacation this summer.

Teacher: You certainly have a lot of lovely pictures.

Kid 3:   I brought a lobster trap. I have lots and lots and lots and lots of stuff to say about lobster traps. (*holds up a thick pile of paper*)

Class: Boring, very boring.

Teacher: Well, you do have a lot of stuff to read. Why don't I take that and read it tonight so we have enough time for the others? Next.

Kid 4:   I brought a video.

Class: There are naked people on it.

Teacher: I'll take that, and we'll watch it ... never.

Kid 5:   This is my daddy's air spray that he uses when he stinks up the bathroom from all the beans and cabbage that he eats. Here, smell this.

Teacher;   That is fine. (*taking the spray can*) That is enough.

Class: Our dads stink too.

Kid 6:   I brought a card.

Teacher: Next.

Kid 7:   I brought my mommy's bra!

Everyone grabs and plays with it, puts in on their heads.

Teacher: Stop that! I'll hold on to this.

Kid 7:   My mommy needs that back.

Teacher: These are for the mommies, not for us.

Kid 8: I brought my mom's lipstick.

Class: It's black lipstick, she must be a witch.

Teacher: I think I'll take that. And her mother is not a witch.

Kid 9: I brought my pet mouse.

Class is upset and screaming. Child taunts the other children and teacher with the mouse. Teacher hates the mouse.

Teacher: (*cowering*) It is perfectly normal to be afraid of something. Perfectly normal.

Kid 10: I brought a bird.

Bird escapes from the cage. Chaos ensues.

Teacher: Oh, I just love my job.

Vignette 10: The Play

Teacher is at centre stage (CS). Kids enter.

Teacher: Welcome to the Shakespeare play auditions. I need your name and then we can continue. OK. Who is first?

Kid 1: I'm _____.

Kid 2: I'm _____.

Teacher: You do realise this is Shakespeare?

Kid 1:   Yes, we are Rosencrantz and Guildenstern. (*They chant.*) To be or not to be, that is the question.

Teacher: Next.

Kid 3:   (*using sign language*) To be or not to be, that is the question.

Teacher: Next.

Kid 4:   To be or not to be, that is the question.

Teacher: Next.

Kid 5:   To be or not to be, that is the question.

Teacher: Louder.

Kid 5:   *(again, just as quiet)*

Teacher: This is the theatre, you need to project.

Kid 5:   (*loudly*) To be or not to be, that is the question.

Teacher: Next.

Kid 6:   I'm going to do Shakespeare in the Garden. (*mimics a bee*) To beeeee or not to beeeeee, that is the question.

Teacher: Next.

Kid 7:   To be or not to be. That is the question.

Teacher: Is there anyone else? Well, you all gave wonderful auditions, and I think we can find a place for everyone of you in our play; it is Shakespeare.

All the kids congratulate each other, excited.

Teacher: Now, we have a lot work to do, so be here on time. Rehearsals begin at

7 a.m.

Kid 1: (*shocked*) I'm not awake at 7. Who'd want to do theatre?

All the actors: (*look at each other and then shout*) We would! We are InsideOut!

THE END

CHAPTER SIX

The Family Portrait

From Performance Lines to Backstage

By the time InsideOut Theatre had presented several successful performances and my confidence in mounting a production grew, I noticed that the audience was shifting from interactive theatre to pure entertainment. The original popular 'sociogram' theatre technique and general interactive audience participation were no longer well received. The audience just wanted to sit back, laugh, and enjoy an evening out.[18] InsideOut actors, too, were restless for change and growth. Original group members wanted to explore new performance venues and, ultimately, formed the Touring Group. It was time to clean up our act. This bold step forward into the realm of theatre was nerve-racking, yet thrilling and inspiring. There was only one omnipresent, overriding philosophical challenge--how to maintain our Feminist approach of inclusion and mutual support while facing a new patriarchal entity, the theatre community.

This notion may seem confusing as theatre artists are typically perceived as unconventional and freethinking.[19] I

---

[18] During a healing séance, Taylor notes, the Shaman "demands that the audience experience 'recreation' a difficult psychological journey, but few people would volunteer for such 'hard times'" (p. 43). "If the people watching the performance are witnesses rather than participants, an audience comes into being (p. 58).

[19] In Roman times, performers were subjected to "harsh and extensive caste-laws and legal prejudices." Despite demands of equality for all, "the French Revolution failed to enfranchise actors and entertainers" (Taylor, p. 65). Even today, a career in the arts is

discovered, however, that this stereotype lies primarily offstage. Onstage, I found mainstream actors tended to embrace a theatrical protocol which was conventional and at times even rigid. Furthermore, a constant jostling for top dog position was evident. From a hierarchical perspective, who was the most important? Was it the actor who presented the script, the script writer, the director who gave the thing shape and appeal, or the heroes of the technical support team, who were unnoticed until something went wrong?

I found the debate quite tiresome and unnecessary. From the perspective of a collective approach, it seemed clear to me that everyone was important and necessary. Theatre companies that possess the resources necessary to fill all theatrical roles are essentially, fortunate.

As the Artistic Director of an expanding alternative theatre company, I wore a multitude of hats: theatrical, therapeutic, supportive, and custodial. I knew instinctively that moving into the theatre community necessitated collaboration with theatre artists, and my initial belief was that there would be fewer patriarchal restrictions than found in the academy. This was somewhat true because not all theatre artists receive formal academic training. To a greater extent, however, the distinctions were minimal. More and more, theatre artists, in an attempt to secure their own futures, find that university degrees help, and the university bias, contrary to popular belief, tends to support the status quo.[20] Over time and as a result of this awareness, I developed a growing appreciation for the diverse and flexible training I

---

not viewed as being as respectable as a career in, say, medicine or law.

[20] Taylor points out, "peoples' entertainment, that constant rival of official displays of power and grandeur, was provided by the travelling players…who had never whole-heartedly entered society… They offer an alternative culture, *a culture counter*, to the official blandishments of civilised society" (p. 62).

received from the Rehabilitation Studies Programme; truly an academic anomaly.

Ironically, *The Family Portrait* was the final performance in the church auditorium by InsideOut Theatre. It was the company's last hurrah as a collective that resembled a family more than a company. The exciting challenge of securing performance venues coupled with learning theatrical jargon entered the scene. The accessibility I had previously enjoyed and had taken for granted became a primary production focus. I was shocked to learn that many public-performing venues were not wheelchair accessible. Some claimed to be accessible but clearly did not have actors in wheelchairs in mind. Wheelchair accessibility was limited to patrons only. Other performing spaces had wheelchair accessible stages but non-accessible dressing rooms and bathrooms. The status of emergency exits was even more startling. I was dismayed to discover how many venues did not offer wheelchair accessible emergency exits, even those newly constructed or recently renovated. There was limited Braille signage, indicating elevators or doors. Talking elevators, so prevalent today, were also non-existent.

Rental fees for many performing venues were a revelation, and threatened the company's dedication to financial accessibility. InsideOut performers and patrons are frequently people with limited finances. Our mission supports theatre accessibility for all. Maintaining nominal registration fees and ticket prices is paramount. Revenue from these sources is typically insufficient for theatre rentals. Constant fund-raising is a result; subsidising production costs.

A final challenge with performing venues emerged from the unorthodox decision by InsideOut not to offer a traditional season. Traditional theatre typically has regular schedules that include several weeks of consecutive performances preceded by several weeks of rehearsal. Performances are scheduled every night of the week except Monday, with the occasional matinee. In contrast, InsideOut performances can happen anytime, anywhere, whenever we have an invitation to perform. As word spread, InsideOut began to receive numerous invitations to perform at conferences, banquets, and events such as volunteer appreciation celebrations. Thus, our rehearsal schedule varied significantly. As a direct result of our company's roots, we rehearse weekly, typically for two hours. Longer rehearsal sessions are not advisable because of actor and facilitator fatigue.

A performance venue offers customary features like a stage and accompanying spaces such as the house, offstage areas, dressing rooms etc. Traditionally, InsideOut used the focal strategy of a performance line where actors sat on a row of chairs facing the audience in a church auditorium. This performance line served as an onstage living backdrop. Actors could move freely in and out of their seats to accommodate the various vignettes. This particular arrangement established the practice of absolute visibility that InsideOut actors enjoy.

To increase the performance focus, we next added a physical backdrop which soon became an essential component of InsideOut performances. As our shows grew increasingly sophisticated, we needed to conceal props and actors not relevant to a particular vignette. Eventually, portable, transferable, and practical backdrops were created in order to accommodate the needs of the Touring Group. Before the final creation, several prototypes were constructed with varying success.

The initial creation worked in conjunction with the performance line and was constructed by group members. Actors lay on large pieces of cardboard while shadowy outlines were drawn and then later filled in using a variety of creative means, such as sponge paint. The end product was effective, but the material was fragile and only lasted one season. The second creation was designed and constructed by a local visual artist. It was sophisticated, mobile, and sturdy, but too large for easy mobility. Our third backdrop was less sophisticated, but extremely portable. It lasted a few seasons before collapsing. Finally, a durable design was constructed where a frame of pipes was embedded in cement blocks from which were hung simple black drapes. It was professional, relatively portable, and, for the most part, has withstood the rigors of touring. Portable backdrops also can be purchased. We rejected this option initially as too costly. In retrospect, when considering the amount of time, energy, and money involved, it would have been a wise investment. Ideally, a backdrop must be assembled and disassembled (struck) in fifteen minutes or less.

It has been said that timing is everything and, no doubt, good timing, from a technical viewpoint, has made for attractive performances. The advent of sophisticated computers, as well as portable CD players, have allowed InsideOut productions to incorporate sound cues but this created a need for sound technicians. Technical support came from students, support partners, the occasional professional, and, as always, InsideOut facilitators. Each stage of the company's evolution has required the acquisition of an additional hat for InsideOut facilitators.

One of the greatest distinctions between InsideOut and traditional theatre is that a theatrical collective requires role flexibility, both on and offstage. A trained InsideOut facilitator develops a keen sense of how to incorporate each actor's idiosyncrasies and mixed abilities into a performance. The patriarchal hierarchical basis of western culture has been challenged by our co-operative approach, especially in the early years of InsideOut's history. Typically, InsideOut facilitators have been contracted employees, who stay long enough to make contributions to the company while learning about our Feminist approach to theatre. Inevitably they take what they have learned and move on to alternative educational, or employment opportunities. As the Artistic Director, this scenario means that constant training and retraining is necessary to sustain the company.[21]

Fortunately, theatre education has evolved and now places greater emphasis on the inherent benefits of the dramatic process for individuals and society at large. Ironically, this trend is not a new phenomenon, but a return to theatre's roots. Historically, theatre was embraced in community settings for its transformative powers, playing an integral part in the community's growth and expression.

"To make the leap from Shaman to superstar we must embark on a strange and enchanting journey. We must engage in that most ancient, rewarding and entertaining of all human endeavours, a journey of the soul."[22] This is what ties theatre work to Shamanism, as described by Taylor: both are transformative to their audiences. It is here that we are reminded of the sacred space wherein 'performance' lives. Whether we are making a distinction between theatre as an art form or as belonging to the people, the fact remains that performance in and of itself is transformative, belonging to the sacred, and inherent in the human condition. In my estimation, the sacred and transformative nature of performance is integral to the human experience; a universal law. Drama has historically possessed transformative powers, [23] but transformation doesn't always happen

---

[21] Taylor connects showbiz, education, and initiation into the sacred mysteries in describing a magic trick in which a child is put into a basket and asked questions by her mentor. When her answers do not please him, he pushes her into the basket and plunges a sword into it, apparently killing the child. The mentor then shows the basket is empty and the child reappears. "The teacher-pupil setting is reinforced by the fact that the sequence of events plainly refers to a kind of *education...*" The initiate must journey through the Underworld, or die, before learning the proper answers. Therefore, the mentor 'kills' her, so that she can be reborn. "Only then will the pupil be truly 'educated'" (p. 133).

[22] Taylor, p. 13.

[23] As a result of persecution, the followers of Shamanism began to

overnight. It has repeatedly been said that an InsideOut performance is its own best promotion because people do leave feeling entertained and substantively informed.[24] Our job is to make it look easy. Sometimes it is easy, sometimes it is riddled with challenge, but it is always a fulfilling test of our creative abilities; just like family!

---

hide their healing séances within the guise of entertainment, producing "a seed, the show that effectively preserved its mystery in a hard shell, which not only protected but also disguised it. Show business is this outer shell…" (Taylor, p. 56).

[24] Taylor observes, "the show is…the outer wrapping on a parcel… [It] amalgamates entertainment with instruction. The audience is educated through the performance, yet still left breathless, wondering how…such things can be done at all" (p. 35).

THE FAMILY PORTRAIT

Tableau

The Family Portrait.

Sad.

I'd rather watch hockey.

I'm putting on my lipstick.

Call it family time.

Oh, no. We're late again, hurry up.

Let's just get this over with.

Oh yea!

I'm missing my nap.

I wanna go outside.

SMILE

Vignette 1

Two women onstage; they are looking at a photo album.

Woman 2:   Oh, I haven't seen this in years. Look at this Christmas picture from 1975.

Woman 1:   Remember how well everyone got along?

Woman 2:   I remember it much differently than that.

Flashback: Phone rings.

Child 1: Hello, yeah, it's me. I'm just waiting. It's going to be hard making it through this family thing.

Mom: Could you help me with dinner?

Child 1: No, I can't. I'm on the phone.

Mom: Could you help me with dinner?

Child 2: No, we're watching TV.

Child 3: Yeah, it's the football game. We don't want to miss it.

Mom: Stupid men running about in skinny little tights. Can you help me with dinner?

Child 4: Give me something to chop.

Mom mimes giving him/her vegetables, cutting board, etc. She/he proceeds to chop slowly.

Mom: No, that's not right. I'll do it myself. No one is doing it right. I'll have to do it by myself to get it done right.

Takes everything back. Mom bustles around.

Mom: Dinner's ready. Come have dinner as a family.

No one pays attention to Mom.

Mom: Yooohoooo. Time for everyone to eat.

Child 2: Let's make this fast.

Mom: Who is going to say grace and bless the spirit of the season?

Child 4: Bless the food.

Mom: Eat everything; there are starving people around the world who need this food.

Child 2: I got to get back to the football game.

Everyone shovels the food in fast and gets up and leaves the table. One child starts to choke. Mom assists her.

Mom: I love these happy family Christmases.

Vignette 2

The two old women are looking at the photo album.

Woman 1:   I'll never forget that one.

Woman 2:   Oh, look! Remember this? We had all just gotten to the church...

Flashback: Church music is heard.

Mom: My baby is getting married. I am so emotional.

Dad: Stop crying.

Guests begin to enter. Wedding March *is played.*

Pastor: Everyone be seated, please. We are gathered together today to join these two people in holy matrimony. If anyone knows why these two should not be married, speak now.

Woman 3:   I know why they shouldn't get married, because he is already married to me.

Bride runs out, crying.

Vignette 3

Old women again, looking at a photo album.

Old 1:   This is her daughter.

Old 2:   We all wish we had a daughter like her.

Old 1:   Not like her sister.

Old 2:   I didn't know she had a sister.

Flashback.

Mom: Hurry up, you are moving too slow.

Daughter 1:   I am hurrying. What is the hurry?

Mom: At least I have one daughter who has accomplished something.

Daughter 1:   Well, I'm pregnant, that's an accomplishment.

Mom: Oh sure, shout it out for the whole world to hear.

Speaker: Welcome to the 1997 graduation awards.

Ruth Bieber

This year we have a new award that we have never presented before because we've never had anyone earn it. This year's over-achiever award goes to Alana.

Alana: Believe in yourself. Thanks to my family, and let's party on.

Sister 1: Excellent! I can do that.

Vignette 4

Old women enter again looking at photo album

Old 1: And here is your aunt's family.

Old 2: That's when they went to Disneyland. They were such a happy family that got along so well.

Old 1: That's not what I heard, listen to this –

Flashback: chairs are arranged to be a car.

Dad: Enters, sits in the driver's seat. He honks the horn and the rest of the family enters – Mom sits next to Dad, the four kids start arguing about who sits where.

Daughter 1: I don't want to sit by you.

Daughter 2: And I don't want to sit by you.

Dad: Come on, son. Sit next to me.

Mom: (*to girls*) Behave! I don't want to tell you again.

Dad: Are we ready for our road trip to Disneyland? Fasten your seatbelts.

Mom: Dear, before we go any further, there is something I need to discuss. Your daughter is driving me to distraction. After this trip is over, I want us to go to family counselling.

Daughter 1:   You can't tell me what to do. You're not my mother. She can't tell me what to do; can she, Dad?

Dad: Aaahhhhh.

Daughter 2:   I want to walk around.

Mom: Here is another thing. I am in the house packing all the supplies for this trip, for your kids and mine, doing all the work, and you are sitting out here in the car beeping away on the horn. I want you to know that you should be more cooperative.

Daughters 1 and 2 tease the smallest daughter.

Son: I have to go to the bathroom. Badly.

Mom: Why didn't you go before we left?

Daughter 3:   I have to go to the bathroom, too.

Mom: Pull into the gas station. I told you guys to go at the house.

Mom, son, and youngest daughter exit.

Daughter 1 hides the youngest daughter's toy.

Daughter 2:   (*whispers*) I'm going to tell.

Dad: Everything OK back there?

Daughters: Yes; fine.

Mom: (*enters with younger children*) We're back, let's get going.

Older daughters continue teasing youngest girl.

Mom: Drive please. That is the last stop until we get there.

Daughter 3:   I forgot my baby doll.

Daughter 1:   It's lost forever. Probably at the gas station.

Daughter 3 starts to cry.

Mom: Turn around, we have to go back. I'll go in and look for it. I want you all to stay here and be quiet. (*exits*)

Daughter 1 teases daughter 3 with the doll.

Mom: (*enters*) I can't find the doll. (*sees doll*) Where did that come from?

All the children begin to fight with each other.

Mom: (*screams*) Quiet! (*children stop fighting*) Now, that's better, just enjoy the scenery. Oh, look we're here. Aaaah, another memorable family road trip.

Vignette 5

Enter two old women looking at a photo album.

Old 1:   They've had their struggles.

Old 2:   Yes, but they've really pulled together.

Old 1:   Well, they did, but after the lawsuit.

Old 2:   Lawsuit?

Flashback

Man is lying dead.

Woman 1:   He's dead. It's so sad.

Woman 2:   What will we do?

Woman 3:   I think we need to see a lawyer.

Woman 1:   (*takes off his ring*) He always promised me this ring.

Woman 2:   That is so disgusting. He always promised me this one.

They begin comparing the rings.

Woman 3:   Mom would roll over in her grave if she knew about this. Besides, he always said he'd leave his rings to *me*.

The three women struggle among themselves for the rings.

Vignette 6

Enter old women looking at the photo album.

Old 1:   I remember this. My aunt and uncle's 50th wedding anniversary.

Old 2: Isn't that the one where Aunty forgot to show up?

Old 1: Yes, she was always forgetting everything.

Flashback

Mom: What a party!

Dad: Yeah, it was a great anniversary.

Daughter: (*enters*) You two kids sure know how to put on a great anniversary party. You guys are just as hot as the day you were married. I've come by to help clean up.

Mom: Thank you, Mary.

Doorbell rings.

Mary: Whoever it is, I'll get rid of them.

MLA: After being such lifelong supporters of the Liberal (*or whichever party is in power*) Party, I am giving you a certificate from the Prime Minister for you.

Mom: There has been a mistake. I've never voted Liberal (*or whatever*).

Dad: And I would never vote for a woman.

MLA: There must be some mistake; is this 1111 –21st Street?

Mom: No.

MLA: Sorry, wrong couple. I'll just take my certificate and leave. (*exits*)

Doorbell rings.

Mary: Hello, Auntie Kay.

Aunt: Hello, Shirley.

Mary: It's Mary. Are you here for the anniversary?

Aunt: Of course.

Mary: Well, you are a day late.

Aunt: (*to Mom*) Happy Birthday.

Mom: It was my anniversary.

Aunt: Where is your husband, Shirley?

Mary: It's Mary, and he died last year, remember?

Aunt: Were my brother and his wife here?

Mom: I didn't see them.

Mary: They've passed away also. Would you all like some tea?

Mom: I think we would all prefer whiskey.

Aunt: Do you still have your cat, Karen?

Mary: My name is Mary, and I've never had a cat.

Aunt: I'd like to stay, but I have to go, as I have another party to go to.

Mom: OK.

Dad: Thanks for coming.

Aunt: And happy birthday.

Mom: Anniversary.

Aunt exits. Mary, Mom, and Dad look at each other.

All: Family!

Vignette 7

Old women looking at photo album.

Old 1:   Do you remember when she had her first child?

Old 2:   How could I forget?

Flashback.

Mom: Darling, she has your eyes.

Dad: Let's name her Mary after my mother.

Mom: OK. Hold her gently. I don't know what to do when she cries.

Dad: I have to go to work tomorrow.

Mom: You can't go. I don't know what to do.

Dad: I'll call my mom, and she can help you with the baby.

Doorbell

Grandma: We are here.

*Baby starts to cry. Grandma picks her up and rocks her.
Baby stops crying.*

Mom: Was she too warm?

Grandma: She needs to have her diaper changed.

Dad: I'd like to go out with my wife, and we are hoping you will look after her for a while.

Grandma: I'm always looking after you guys!

Mom: I know, but will you stay and help?

Grandma: Well, I wouldn't leave her alone!

Vignette 8

Enter old women looking at photo album.

Old 1: Look, a picture of Karen and her daughter, Selma.

Old 2: Where is she in the photo?

Old 1: (*pointing at the photo*) Oh yes, she had a tendency to wander.

Flashback

Mom: OK, Selma, this shopping trip will be quick. Stay near me all the time.

Selma: OK, mommy.

Mom: I want to try on this outfit, and I want you to stay right here. You listen.

Selma wanders off.

Mom: (*squeezes into skirt*) Selma. Selma. Selma! Sir, have you seen my daughter?

Man: No.

Mom: (*to woman*) Have you seen my daughter? I can't find her.

Woman: No, I haven't seen her.

Mom: (*upset*) Someone has to help me.

Mom paces back and forth, crying.

Manager: (*enters with Selma*) Come with me; your mom wants you.

Selma: I don't talk to strangers. (*starts to call for her mother*)

Mom: I have been looking all over for you!

Mom and Selma begin to leave.

Manager: You are leaving with the skirt.

Mom: Oh, I'm sorry, I am so flustered.

Manager: Another day in Shop Eazy.

Vignette 9

Enter two old women looking at photo album.

Old 1:   There is a picture of the family picnic.

Old 2:   What a lot of photos they took that day.

Old 1:   And everyone looks wet.

Flashback: people enter running and happy about a picnic.

Daughter 2:   Let's sit here. This is a good spot.

Mom: This looks nice.

Daughter 1:   Let's go exploring.

Daughter 2:   Yeah.

Dad is taking photos.

Daughter 1:   I hate it when he takes these stupid photos.

Daughter 2:   I'm in the water, and Dad is taking pictures.

Mom: She's cold, get her out of there.

Daughter 2:   I don't want to.

Daughter 1:   You're turning blue!

Mom: I think we had better go home.

Dad continues to take pictures throughout.

Vignette 10

Enter two old women looking at photo album.

Old 1:   Oh, here is a picture of Ruth with her daughters.

Old 2:   Well, they look like they are having fun.

Old 1:   But what happened to her feet?

Flashback

Ruth: I have just had the worst day of my entire life. I don't want to talk about it, think about it, or see anyone, or do anything. I just want to sit here alone in the peace and quiet and experience my migraine.

Girls: Hi, Mom, why don't you play with us?

Ruth: No, I have a headache, and I don't want to be bothered.

Girls: You don't want to be bugged?

Ruth: No, vamoose.

Girls: I know what we can get for her – her slippers.

Ruth: Good, go get them. (*aside*) They will never find those slippers.

Girls: We found them.

Ruth: How did you do that?

Girls begin to tease their mother with the slippers.

Ruth: I know you want me to chase you, but I am not going to do that.

Girls continue to tease the mother.

Ruth: (*stands up and chases the girls*) Oh, you two! When I am feeling bad, you just make everything better by making me laugh.

Vignette 11

Enter two old women looking at photo album.

Old 1:   The last picture in the book was taken on her 20th birthday.

Old 2:   She sure looks surprised, doesn't she?

Old 1:   You have no idea, see; she went to the café –

Flashback, people sitting and drinking.

Girl 1:   Hi, guys, good to see you.

The people ignore her.

Girl 1:   Hey, you guys, talk to me, I don't understand. It's my birthday, and nobody is talking to me. (*aside*) I should have stayed home and talked to my cat. Not one of my friends was available to hang out with me on my birthday. None of them remembered. Maybe I should just go home and feed the cat.

Entire cast sneaks up and yells "Surprise" and sings Happy Birthday.

THE END

Ruth Bieber

CHAPTER SEVEN

Advocacy in Action

InsideOut Becomes Incorporated

Prior to the InsideOut initiative separating from the Rehabilitation Studies Programme at the University of Calgary, I realised the project would require funding. This was early in the history of InsideOut and I was still enjoying the financial security of my job as a counselling therapist. Unbeknownst to me, changes were imminent. Theatre arts for populations with disabilities were clearly becoming the passionate core of my career but the arduous work of fund-raising was diverting my time and energy from the creative heart of the company. Initially, a graduate practicum student researched small project grant opportunities, and found that in order to receive government funding, we needed charitable status. The company could accept donations if we could issue receipts for tax deduction. Thus began the challenging two-year process toward legal sovereignty.

Obtaining charitable status was a two-step process involving acceptance, by first the provincial government, and then the federal government. I was surprised to discover that the two levels of government were not coordinated and this led to confusion and delays. Many application forms boomeranged among the offices before InsideOut was able to provide tax-deductible receipts for donations. Years later, our charitable status was useful for lottery funding applications.

Another condition we had to meet was the establishment of a Board of Directors. At minimum, this Advisory Board included a President, a Vice-President, a Treasurer, and a Secretary whose primary functions were signing authority and accounting services. We eventually acquired the services of a chartered accountant, who became invaluable as the requirements of funding agencies grew more stringent. The need for an audited annual financial statement, once a rarely requested document, is now commonplace. As the company evolved, the Board has assumed a larger governance role by developing a strategic plan and vision statement, while also overseeing some day-to-day operations. Due to increased responsibility, the Board researched liability insurance for its members, something not previously considered. Several of my faithful friends and colleagues have served as Board members over the years, providing voluntary expertise in specialized areas like promotions.

Working with a Board of Directors can be a complex undertaking. On the one hand, a Board of Directors can support daily operations to varying degrees, which provides relief to the working staff. On the other hand, being responsible to a Board of Directors, can also add to the work load of an artistic director. Like many Artistic Directors and association coordinators, I had been managing the administrative duties myself. After incorporation, this was no longer possible; hence, the addition of a paid administrative assistant.

The company was incorporated as "The Association of the InsideOut Integrated Theatre Project." This legal name accommodates all the necessary incorporation requirements, as does the Mission Statement: *To enable participants with disabilities to enjoy, participate in, and benefit from the development of a training program and participation in the same, culminating in a theatre production.* The mission statement focuses primarily on artistic expression. Incorporation, over all enhances one of the company's key mandates; advocacy.

ADVOCACY IN ACTION

Enter cast, signing and singing the song.

Song: We are climbing the ladder to a better way –

Facilitator: Everybody stand up and join us to learn how to both sing this song and

sign it.

Tableau

Advocacy!!!!

Rallies.

Not guilty.

Government.

Insubordination.

Power.

ADVOCACY!!!

Vignette 1

Connie: How ya doing?

Pam: Fine. Give me five.

They look for the train.

Pam: Oh, man, I hate waiting for the train. It's so boring.

Connie: Check it out. (*motions to the people with disabilities on the platform*)

Pam: Oh, wow, let's have some fun.

Connie: Weirdo, weirdo, loser.

Andy: Go away.

Pam: Let's push them off the bridge. Let's scare them.

Beth: Leave us alone.

Authority   What is going on here?

Pam: Party-pooper.

Authority: (*to Pam and Connie*) If necessary, I can phone the police. (*to the people with disabilities*) Listen, you two, there is some back up, if you are ever hassled again. See this button here? In emergencies only, you can push this and help will come.

Andy: That's great. Thanks so much.

Authority: And for now, I am just going to hang out with you until the train comes to make sure you aren't hassled again.

Beth: Thanks.

Train goes by. Everyone leaves on board except the bullies.

Pam: Fine, I wanted to walk.

Connie: Me too.

Vignette 2

Selma enters looking cold and alone. She is begging for money.

Anne enters and looks disturbed and irritated by the begging person. Anne uses the ATM. Enter another person begging. Anne exits, avoiding them both.

Selma discovers that Anne has forgotten her money at the ATM. Takes the money.

Anne: (*returns, sees Selma with the money and calls*) Police!

Police constable enters.

Anne: See, she is stealing my money!

Police take Selma away.

Vignette 3

Judge: This court is in session. Next case, please.

Prosecutor: This person stole money. She claims it was to feed her children.

Judge: She took money she found at an ATM? And how do you plead?

Selma: Not guilty.

Judge: Do you have a defence counsel? And would they

please present their case?

Counsel: This woman is new to Calgary, and she is not familiar with the services.

Prosecutor: Objection, lack of familiarity is not an excuse.

Lawyer: She is very sorry that she took the money, but she was desperate. She didn't know what else to do. We should let this woman off with some community service to repay her debt. She really needs help.

Judge: Very well, thank you. Prosecution, state your case.

Prosecutor: Ladies and gentlemen of the jury, taxpaying Calgarians. Of course, the defendant is sorry; after all, she got caught. I implore you, is this the type of example we want to set for our children? That criminal behaviour is practically given a slap on the wrist at best? I think not. Do we want the entire backwash from all parts of Canada seeping into our city because they know they can get away with crimes? And furthermore your honour, ladies, and gentlemen, she is a person with a disability, and how many people with disabilities are productive members of society anyway? I say we should make an example of this case. Put her children into foster care where we know they will be properly taken care of.

Judge: Ladies and gentlemen of the court, I would like to open up this discussion to you in case there are any arguments we may have missed. Would anyone like to comment?

Voice 1:   She has committed a crime. Throw her in the clink.

Voice 2:   She deserves a second chance.

Judge: Anyone else? Very well, thank you, I've made a decision. She is guilty of taking money she found at an ATM, and I am going to give her a suspended sentence, in which she will do community service to repay what she has taken. Furthermore I'll assign her an advocate to help her through the social system so that she can become, as she is no doubt capable, a useful member of society.

Prosecutor: Bleeding heart liberal.

Vignette 4

Knocking on door.

Pastor: Hello, come on in. You are…

Connie: Connie.

Henry: Henry.

Pastor: Welcome to the church of Bliss and Joy. What can I do for you today?

Connie: We would like to join the premarital seminal.

Pastor: Oh, you mean the premarital seminars. We are well noted for our seminars. You wish to get married?

Henry: Yes.

Pastor: When you called you indicated you have disabilities.

Connie: Yes, but we take care of ourselves.

Pastor: Well, yes, I am sure you do, and that is very admirable; however, I should get a signature from your legal guardians giving consent.

Connie: We don't have guardians. We take care of ourselves.

Pastor: I am sure in a way you do, but we don't want anything to clutter up the process, so just bring in your legal guardians, and we can continue this discussion.

Connie: Maybe we should bring in our parents.

Pastor: That would be lovely.

Connie: We'll be back.

Knocking at door.

Pastor: Well, that was fast, come right on in. Everyone please sit down.

Father: I'm Henry's father.

Mother: I'm Connie's mother.

Pastor: I'm not sure if you are aware of this, but Connie and Henry have come to me asking to become enrolled in our premarital seminar.

Mother: Sounds great. Put them in, please.

Pastor: Perhaps you wouldn't mind signing this form as their legal guardians.

Mother: Perhaps I would mind signing that form. They are their own guardians, and they can make this decision.

Pastor: Really.

Connie: Yes, Henry and I have been living together for five years. We have our own apartment and jobs.

Pastor: In a sheltered workshop.

Connie: No, I've been working in the same restaurant for seven years, and Henry has been working in a factory for five years.

Pastor: What a great work record. So, as a show of good faith, I would like your parents to sign this.

Mother: I happen to be a lawyer, and I will not sign this.

Pastor: Fine. Will you fax the information to me so that I can show it to my trustees? (*to Connie and Henry*) And as for you two, I guess I'll see you in class on Tuesday.

Vignette 5

Waitress: Welcome to the Greasy Spoon. Here are your menus; anything to drink?

Person 1: Soda.

Person 2: Root beer.

Enter two other patrons.

Person 3: I do not know why we have to keep trying out new restaurants because you like a change.

Person 4: I don't like to always eat in places where I have the menu memorised.

Person 3: I like it when I know what a place offers and

what to expect. This is so embarrassing.

Person 4:   This is called self-advocacy. Stretch yourself.

Waitress: Welcome to the Greasy Spoon. Do you want anything to drink?

Person 4:   Do you have any soft drinks?

Waitress: They are all listed there in the menu in black and white.

Person 4:   We have a little bit of trouble reading.

Waitress: I'll give you time to think about it. It's all there in bold letters.

Person 3:   See what I mean?

Person 4:   Oh, don't be daunted.

Person 4:   Are there any pictures to go by?

Person 3:   No, except for the chocolate sundae.

Person 4:   They've always got pictures of dessert.

Waitress: Have you decided what you'll have?

Person 1:   I'll have the fish and chips special.

Person 2:   Hamburger, french fries, and my drink.

Waitress: Gravy with the fries?

Person 2:   Yes.

Person 3:   Hey, we know that they have fish and chips, hamburgers, and fries.

Person 4:   I am a strict vegetarian. That information does me no good whatsoever.

Person 3:   Me either.

Waitress: Have you decided what you would like to eat?

Person 3:   Do you have any vegetarian meals?

Waitress: Right there on the menu.

Person 3:   As I mentioned before, we have trouble reading the menu, so if you could just list the meals for us.

Waitress: I am a bit busy, and don't have time for that, so I will give you another minute to choose, and I'll be right back.

Person 3:   Guess you were right. This is going nowhere fast.

Person 1:   Excuse me, I just noticed that the waitress wasn't very helpful to you, so I thought I would come by and offer some assistance.

Person 3:   Thank you, she just really doesn't get it. Do they have any vegetarian meals?

Person 1:   Yes, they have some vegetarian lasagne and some stir-fries.

Waitress: Is there a problem here?

Person 3:   This kind patron here is assisting us with the menu, which you were unwilling to do.

Waitress: As you can no doubt see, I have tons of customers waiting for service. My section is full, and my job is not to babysit you.

Person 3:   That's it, I've had enough. We are leaving.

Waitress: You already have your beverages; you have to pay for them.

Person 3:   Take them out of your salary.

Person 1:   You know, I've seen enough, we are going, too.

Person 3:   Hey, do you want to join us at our regular spot? The service is great there.

Person 1:   You're on.

Waitress: Disabled people are such a problem!

Vignette 6

Person 1:   (*wearing a large backpack*) Hi. You waiting for the bus?

Person 2:   Yep, the #9. I am heading up to Bridgeland.

Person 1:   Do you live up there?

Person 2:   Yep, I've got a nice apartment there. It's a good place; the government helps me pay part of the rent.

Person 1:   I could use a place like that.

Person 2:   Why don't you come by and see it? Then maybe something could work for you.

Person 1:   Could I come now?

Person 2:   Sure, and here's the bus.

Enter apartment.

Person 2:   Come on in, my place is great – big bathroom, bedroom, living room with kitchenette.

Person 1:   It's wonderful.

Person 2:   Want something to drink?

Person 1:   Sure.

Person 2:   I've got orange juice.

Person 1:   Anything else?

Person 2:   Nope, just that.

Person 1:   OK. Orange juice sounds great.

(*Person 2 exits and Person 1 starts miming that she is taking all his stuff and putting it into her back pack. She stops when Person 2 returns.*)

Person 2:   (*starts talking offstage and enters*) So, this place is great. Good view.

Person 1:   I think I will talk to your landlord and see if I can get a place here. Where is your landlord?

Person 2:   Down the hall in number 3.

(*Person 1 exits with backpack.*)

Person 2:   That would be great if she lived here. I'd have a friend. I think I'll heat up my coffee in the...hey, what happened to my microwave...and my radio...and my clock? What's going on? God, it couldn't have been that girl! What about my fifty bucks I had in this drawer? Shit, she took that too. She stole all my stuff. I'll phone Henry – unless she stole the phone, too – he'll help me.

Person 2:   Hey, Henry? I have some bad news here. This stranger came to my home and stole a bunch of stuff from me. What am I going to do?

Henry: Sounds like what happened to me. I'll arrange a meeting tonight for 7:00 with an advocate that can talk to us and then get back to you.

Person 2:   Great! Henry is on it. A meeting.

Later at 7:00 p.m. meeting in Person 2's apartment. Everyone discussing the description of the person who was in their homes and what she has stolen.

Henry: This is my friend, Lonnie, who is an advocate, and she can help us with this problem we are all having.

Person 2:   Can we get our stuff back?

Advocate: Well, we can try. We've got a security guard, and he thinks we should put up some surveillance cameras. But then the rent will go up. Also, we could call the police and file our own reports.

General: Let's take it into our own hands; find the girl, and beat her up.

Advocate: Hold on, we want to do things the right way, or we'll end up in trouble. There are more positive ways to solve this. We've already got a description, and we've given it to the police.

General: Guess we shouldn't let strangers into our apartments, even if they are really friendly.

General: How about a block watch?

Person 1 enters stage walking down the corridor outside the apartment.

General: Hey, there she is. Grab her. Get her! (*Everyone runs off to grab her.*)

Advocate: Hey, wait. This isn't advocacy. Ah, well, back to the drawing board.

Intermission

Vignette 7

Bunch of actors quacking and acting like ducks in the park.

Ducks: We're hungry, where is bagel man? He is usually here by noon. We have to do something about him.

New Duck: Hi, I just flew in from Edmonton, and are my wings ever tired!

Ducks: Drink the water.

New Duck: (*drinks water, spits it out.*) Yuck.

Ducks: Here comes bagel man!! Yippee!!

Man feeds ducks.

Woman: Hi, there, I've noticed that you have been feeding the ducks every day, and I was wondering if you noticed the sign that says "Do Not Feed the Ducks?"

Man: What?

Woman: I know that you are trying to be kind, but you are not really, because if you feed them, they won't fly south for the winter, and if they don't do that, it'll mess up their whole system. Also, you are feeding them bagels, and they don't have much nutritional value. Clogs up their systems.

Ducks: (*to woman*) Hey, stop it, you. (*to man*) Don't listen to her!

Woman: Anyways, it would be much better if you didn't feed the ducks.

Man: OK, I'll stop. I just didn't think.

Woman: How about a coffee?

Man: OK.

Ducks: What? What? Come back…

Irate flurry of wings and ducks.

Vignette 8

Coach 2: So how do you feel about coaching these lovely young skaters?

Coach 1: Great.

Coach 2: Yeah, you've been at if for almost thirty years; seems about time for you to retire. But you are a very seasoned coach. (*Skaters line up and cross their arms.*) Oh, look at them. Henry, can I help you?

Henry: I am tired of this music.

Person 1: This is the classics.

Henry: Well, I'm bored with it.

Coach 1: Well, you are the only one, because every one else loves it.

Skaters: No, we are all sick of it. It's boring music.

Coach 1: Coach, tell them, it's great.

Skaters: It sucks. We want rock and roll.

Coach 1: You can't skate to rock and roll.

Skaters: We want change. We want good music.

Coach 1: These guys are self-advocating. Should we put on rock and roll?

Coach 2: Yes.

Music cue: rock and roll.

Everyone starts to dance and have a great time.

Vignette 9

Person 1: Why do we keep coming back to this restaurant?

Person 2: I can smell something really bad. Like a smelly dog?

Person 1: There is a dog in here. I can smell it.

Waitress: Welcome to the Greasy Spoon restaurant. Welcome back.

Person 1: Yes, we are back.

Waitress: Here are your menus. What would you like to drink?

Person 1: Decaffeinated coffee.

Waitress: Yes, we have decaffeinated.

Person 2: Water.

Waitress: OK. Are you sure?

Person 2: Last time they gave me caffeinated coffee.

Person 1: Excuse me, waitress, those people have brought a dog into the restaurant.

Waitress: I'll talk to the manager.

Person 1:   She should know dogs are not allowed in the restaurant.

Manager: Is everything to your liking?

Person 1:   No, there is a smelly dog in your restaurant.

Manager: No! Really? I'll go deal with this. Excuse me, ma'am. Health regulations do not allow dogs in restaurants. You must leave.

Person 3 mimes that she is Deaf, and the dog hears for her.

Manager: (*to waitress*) Paper and pen, immediately. (*writes while speaking aloud*) Sorry, you cannot hear, but you cannot have a dog in the restaurant.

Person 3 passes a sheet of paper.

Manager: This is a certificate for a hearing dog?

Person 1:   A hearing dog? Next thing you know we will have scenting dogs, feeling dogs, speaking dogs.

Manager: (*to waitress*) Waitress, I guess you have to take her order. (*to original couple*) I am so sorry, but it appears that this dog is a "hearing dog," and he hears for the Deaf lady. I am terribly sorry. Would you like another table?

Person 1:   And they get all the good parking spots, too.

Waitress: I'll be right back with your order.

Dog suddenly gets up, barks, and drags its owner offstage.

Person 1.   Well, how rude? Is that dog going in the kitchen?

Sound cue: high-pitch beep from malfunctioning smoke alarm.

Person 1:   Now what? A fire? Let's get out of here!

Manager: I told you to replace the battery in the fire alarm! Stupid waitress.

Person 2:   It was the dog. The dog heard the beeping first and tried to warn us. What a wonderful animal. Thank you so much. The dog is welcome anytime.

Vignette 10

Music cue: game show theme music. The host stands at a podium, and when the contestant enters, she joins him. There is a row of squares on the floor, each with a number and a corresponding resource person.

Cue person: Let's Get Service. Take One.

Host: Welcome, studio audience, to another exciting show of "Let's Get Service."
One lucky studio audience member can win services from the Alberta Government. Now, for the moment you have all been waiting for… Our lucky contestant is Selma!

(*Selma enters*)

Host: Selma, welcome to our program. Are you excited?

Selma: I am very excited.

Host: Before we get to know you a little bit better, I would like to introduce our dice roller, Jamie. (*Jamie takes a bow.*) Now, Selma, why don't you tell the studio audience and everyone in TV-land a little bit about you and why you hope to get Alberta government services for a year?

Selma: My family and I just moved here from B.C. We are down to our last resources, and I am really hoping for services to help us get established in a new life here in Calgary.

Host: Did I not see you on the TV news regarding an ATM theft?

Selma: Nope, not me, but I have been begging for money.

Host: Coincidence, I guess. Now, to begin the program... Jamie, roll that dice.

Jamie: Two!

Host: And we have ... counselling!!!

Counsellor: (*enters*) How can I help you?

Selma: What can you do for me?

Counsellor: I help with emotional problems. Stress in your life?

Selma: I don't understand.

Counsellor: I can give you somebody to talk to.

Selma: Oh, OK, to make me feel better. OK. I understand. So that is what counselling is? I could use some help. I need a place to live, my kids fight all the time, we are feeling rather isolated, and my husband is a lazy bum who sits at home watching TV. I don't know what to do.

Counsellor: How much money do you have?

Selma: Why?

Counsellor: Counselling costs $100.00 an hour.

Selma: I only have five bucks, and that's for groceries.

Counsellor: You can have three free sessions.

Selma: I just moved here from B.C. I have no place to live. We are cold and starving.

Counsellor: I understand, but there are other people ahead of you. Here, fill out these several forms, and maybe we can help you.

Host: How do you feel about that, studio audience?

Audience: Boooo.

Host: Not very helpful. Let's roll again.

Jamie: Six!

Host: And we have... GIMP! Guaranteed Income for the Minority Person!

GIMP: Hi.

Selma: I am completely broke. My family is on the street. We are hungry.

GIMP: Fill out these forms and these forms and then these forms.

Selma: I have some copies of my forms from B.C.

GIMP: No good, you have to fill out the Alberta forms.

Selma: OK, so B.C. and Alberta have completely different rules and regulations. So, OK. I'll fill out these forms. Can I get some money quickly?

GIMP: Yes, in a couple of months.

Selma: Will you help me fill out the forms?

GIMP: No, I am far too busy.

Host: What do you think, studio audience?

Audience: Boooo.

Host: Not doing too well on the game board, but boy, you are collecting forms! Roll that dice. Two again! It's Recreation.

Recreation: Well, we've got all kinds of programs. We have adult and children's programs. Do you have children?

Selma: I would love for my two kids to get involved.

Recreation: We have day camps, swimming lessons, figure skating, and all kinds of things. What do your kids like to do?

Selma: Good choices, but I would love for them to go to day camp and meet other kids and make new friends.

Recreation: How old are your kids?

Selma: Six and nine.

Recreation: We have some good camps for both those ages. They are in separate camps, but they are fun. And what about you? What are you interested in? We have a crocheting course, figure skating, ceramics, bowling.

Selma: But I am feeling rather pudgy lately. Anything more athletic?

Recreation: Yes, we have yoga, aquasize, bowling, but we have a very long waiting list. If you fill out all these forms, we'll call you when we have a space available.

Audience: Booooo.

Host: Your name is going on an awful lot of lists, Selma. But, you have one more chance to win on "Let's Get Service." Jamie, roll the dice.

Jamie: Nine!

Host: And we have... Residential Support Agent.

Residential steps forward.

Selma: I need a place to live.

Residential: How much money do you have available?

Selma: We have no money.

Residential: How about shared accommodation with another family?

Selma: That doesn't sound like a good idea. Kids will

fight…different rules…

Residential: Two for one, double up. Save your money. You can deal with the problems as they come about.

Selma: I guess it is better than nothing – if the other family is a good family. As long as there is respect for our rules and priorities. Maybe they will become friends. OK, how do I get started?

Residential: OK, it might take a couple of months, but here are some forms for you to fill out. That is, if your GIMP is in place.

Selma: But I am still filling out their forms, and that will take a few months.

Audience: Boooooo.

Host: Selma, I don't think you did very well on today's episode of "Let's Get Service."

Selma: I did get lots of forms.

Host: You know what they say, the job's not finished until the paper work is done.

Selma: I understand.

Host: I am sorry you didn't get any service on today's show. But as a consolation prize, I would like to award you an "advocate."

Selma: Yippee……..

THE END

Ruth Bieber

CHAPTER EIGHT

Millennium Dreams and *Help Unwanted*

InsideOut goes on Tour

"Follow Your Bliss" - Joseph Campbell

While our production *Millennium Dreams* celebrated our past by compiling our favourite vignettes, the turning of the millennium brought exciting shifts and changes in the evolution of InsideOut Theatre. I was invited to present my work with InsideOut at the bi-annual High Beam Festival in Adelaide, Australia, where the artistic accomplishments of artists with disabilities were showcased. This was my first experience with an International Arts Festival for people with disabilities.

Several theatre companies were represented globally, and for the first time, I experienced a sense of camaraderie and belonging. Here was an international community that understood the importance of artistic expression for all members of society. The real inspiration arose from the sense of pride and empowerment I felt as a person with a disability. Initially there was the arts community; next, the community of disability culture. Now these two communities were coming together as the disability arts community; people with and without disabilities working together with a common goal.

This is not to imply that all artists at the festival agreed with each philosophical and theoretical premise. There were as many opinions as there were artists, but one of the main areas of debate stemmed from the right to be creative and artistic. Some maintained to be artistic is to be undefined; the 'anything goes' motto. Others felt a strong sense of obligation and commitment toward audience entertainment. True to form, InsideOut holds to a flexible perspective encompassing both sides of the debate; we value audience entertainment, while allowing creative expression for our actors.

I returned from Australia with a renewed commitment to my vision. Fortunately, this coincided with the advent of the term Disability Theatre.[25] I had been doing the work for over seven years and had just called it theatre, not Disability Theatre.

I had always valued working with the community, but at this juncture, began to appreciate what this meant. After all, there are several communities with dynamic connections. There is the disability community, the artistic community, the disability arts community, and, finally, the larger community, otherwise known as the general public. Moreover, within each, lies sub-communities: human services professionals, family members, actors, playwrights, producers, directors, and technicians, just to name a few. As the Artistic Director of a Disability Theatre company, I have discovered that the role of diplomat is surpassed only by that of resource coordinator.

---

[25] I suspect that, one day, we will revert to just calling it "theatre" again, but for the time being I very much appreciate acknowledgment of the reality that people with disabilities can be artists too. Perhaps using the term "Disability Theatre" is actually a way of rehabilitating society into this awareness. Taylor provides an excellent statement about the link between language and culture. "As far as we can tell, it was man's ability to make and use tools which marked the great change from animal into human being...Our tools are our culture...But not all of our first tools were solid objects...One of our most important tools was completely invisible. It was language" (pp. 14–15).

When I returned from the festival, three of these communities, each with its own unique set of circumstances, required my focused attention. The disability community needed to learn the importance of artistic expression, the theatre community required information so as to appreciate the artistic contributions of people with disabilities, and the general public couldn't understand what all the fuss was about, especially in Alberta with its conservative political climate.

I still hear the plaintive words of my dear father, a proud rural Albertan for most of his adult years, repeatedly asking, "What is it you do again?" I could feel a paradigm shift occurring, nevertheless, as myths and discriminatory practices were dismantled and replaced by bridges of awareness and understanding. In this climate, InsideOut forged ahead, undaunted into the public domain.

Touring

"What you see is what you get."

Many theatre companies claim to offer performing opportunities to people with disabilities. Some of these companies employ clever technical supports that promote the theatre production, while camouflaging 'Disability'. InsideOut Theatre, however, believes in the fundamental right of visibility. I advocate the degree to which people with disabilities are allowed to perform on theatrical stages and this reflects the degree to which minorities are allowed to participate on life's stage. For this reason, we rarely camouflage our actors, safeguarding their visibility and avoiding tokenism. We are Disability Theatre and proud of it.[26]

---

[26] Taylor quotes John Lennon: "I've been across to the other side.

The advent of public performance for InsideOut Theatre was exciting, nerve-wracking and encumbered by steep learning curves. As Artistic Director, I was about to experience an expansion in my already overflowing role as caretaker. Adding to the mix, as a disabled company member myself, I was pushed beyond my comfort zone of familiar surroundings. I was now faced with my own physical dependence on caretakers. Fortunately, the supportive model of theatre training, as dictated by Feminist philosophy, was entrenched. We simply needed to bring InsideOut Theatre's training philosophy to the touring domain.

Did we make mistakes? Did we do things once and vow we would never do them again? Absolutely! Historically, as a culture, we were nomads who roamed the country in groups. Today, however, we have become sedentary, so touring presents new challenges. When touring was first entertained with InsideOut Theatre, we assumed that the practical requirements would be minimal. As there were few props and basic costuming, we thought travel would be easy. We had a lot to learn.

For starters, 'recruitment' became an issue; bringing new perspective. Before taking our show on the road to perform for public audiences, I was hesitant and sceptical about recruiting performers. My hesitancy stemmed from a deep philosophical conviction and fundamental desire to ensure on-going participation of the individuals for whom InsideOut Theatre began. I was certain that recruitment would ultimately lead to the elimination of the artists with profound disabilities simply because it is generally easier to work with higher-functioning actors.

There were moments of enlightenment that caused a significant shift in my thinking. First, all InsideOut training programs culminate in a final performance resulting in a

---

/I've shown you everything. I've got nothing to hide."

broad range of performing opportunities for actors. Next, while touring, a fine balance must be maintained between the needs of each actor and the supports available to accommodate these needs. Finally, not every actor can commit to the challenges inherent in touring and public performance; many discover that the glory of being onstage is only one aspect of touring. Here I revisit pertinent information leading up to our first touring experience.

In January 2001, InsideOut performed in a local theatre festival, The High Performance Rodeo. In the months that followed, this same performance was presented, by invitation, to a number of local groups, and also at our first fund-raiser dinner theatre. I learned that the company could deliver the same performance for about two years before the public is saturated. This cycle leads to an inherent challenge: how to accommodate the comings and goings of actors and facilitators over a two year time frame. Virtually all InsideOut Theatre company members have other jobs and use their acting earnings as an income supplement. This financial reality and the ever-changing schedules of members lead to constant shifting and changing within a production. As a result, I began to value recruitment, and sought individuals who could maintain a commitment to a long term touring schedule. Even so, it was rare for two consecutive performances to be delivered by the same body of actors.

In 2001 we began attending Arts Festivals that required out of province travel. The funds raised from the first dinner theatre provided entrance to an International Arts Festival in Vancouver, Kick StArt, held that fall. By the end of 2001, the touring company had learned many things about taking our show on the road. A real turn of events, however, was to occur during the following summer with a Fringe Festival tour in Saskatoon, Edmonton, and Calgary. Despite the excitement, the opportunities for learning, the fodder for oft repeated stories and material for vignettes, we overwhelmingly vowed never to repeat this scenario. Many times, I have been exhausted and worn to the core but that

September, post-tour, stands out. If it did not take the whole cake, it certainly took a very big chunk.[27]

Even under the most favourable circumstances, touring and performing demand much of the human spirit and are not for the faint of heart. In one case, however, a difficult situation became material for a new vignette, fondly referred to as 'The Vacuum Scene'. This vignette made it into our next production titled *Help Unwanted* and came directly from the Saskatoon Fringe tour experience.[28]

The company members who attended the Saskatoon Fringe Festival were a motley crew of four adult actors with disabilities: two with developmental disabilities, one with dual diagnoses, and the other with traumatic brain injury.[29] One artist possessed limited verbal skills, another had limited mobility skills, one had a perceptual disability that caused difficulty with spatial directions, and the fourth artist possessed a negative attitude towards everything. This negativity presented the biggest stumbling block: as stated in the disability rights community, "Attitudes are the real disabilities." All the actors required twenty-four hour

---

[27] As Taylor observes: "A settled way of life and a reasonably certain source of food [and other comforts] have obvious attractions. In contrast, nomadic life is honed down…it can be a hard, unpredictable mode of existence" (pp. 50–51).

[28] The original title of this performance was "Death by Assistance." The theme of this production was that of a light-hearted poke at well-intentioned helpers who, ultimately, were not very helpful. Our flyer captions clearly pointed to this theme, but many potential audience members didn't read past the title, and assumed that it was about assisted suicide. InsideOut productions were not unaccustomed to using dark humour, but, if not handled carefully, this brand of humour can alienate audiences. I decided to change the title to Help Unwanted, which seemed to encourage readers to read on.

[29] Descriptive details have been intentionally altered to protect confidentiality.

custodial support that included meals, laundry, wake-up calls, transportation, and free time activities. There were further challenges in our complex scenario due to actor/facilitator concerns. Two facilitators had little previous experience as caretakers. One facilitator with natural caretaking abilities, but who had never before left her own children, threatened to return home early in the tour. Another actor/facilitator was the support partner of one of the adult actors. She no doubt returned home exhausted, and left the company after the tour. As an aside, there was a working dog in training who was of no practical use to any member of the company, but did manage to take a minor role in the production.

A total of nine company members drove in a cramped van to Saskatoon. A tenth person, the support partner of one of the actors, had been expected but did not show up. Without the balancing factor of this partner, everyone's nerves were frayed by the end. On the final morning, we rose early to make the seven-hour trek home. Everyone was to pack the night before, with assistance if necessary, so we could leave promptly at eight A.M. One particular actor, who prided himself on being independent, insisted he would be ready to go. The time for final room check arrived and, to our amazement, his room was scattered with toiletries, crumpled clothing, various odd-looking things, and, to our chagrin, vomit. The brave soul had been sick during the tour but not wanting to be a bother, did not tell anyone. His belongings were quickly gathered into a large garbage bag and tossed into the back of the van. This was one load of laundry that was going home.

The performance vignette that developed from this travel experience elicited robust laughter, and a therapeutic effect. It was therapeutic for the audience because laughter and commiseration are good for the soul, and it was therapeutic for the actors because we were able to take this horrendous touring experience onto the stage, and then laugh at it ourselves. [30]

Reflecting upon the challenges of our three-city, fringe touring experience the summer of 2002, the decision was unanimous; InsideOut would never repeat the scenario. The greatest challenge was a lack of commitment from company members to the entire tour. Actors, facilitators, and support partners came and went (or threatened to leave) for a variety of interesting reasons, including family vacation, wedding plans, pet sitting, a breakdown of a guardian-actor relationship, and conflict with work schedules. None of these reasons related to the tour Itself, but the uncertainty created by a constantly shifting company membership made my job much more difficult. I can be proud, though, of managing a successful three-city Fringe Festival tour under the most extraordinary circumstances. There was only one complaint about tour events, which turned out to be a misunderstanding. One actor lamented that the facilitators were going to the pub, while leaving the actors with disabilities to fend for themselves in residence. This complaint was untrue but points to the second greatest challenge faced on the tour; the lack of free time for those responsible for the safety, well-being, and enjoyment of the group. Clearly, had there been opportunity for regular breaks from the rigours of custodial care and production duties, nerves would have been spared and tensions decreased. This aspect of the InsideOut experience is one

---

[30] Traditionally, according to Taylor, humans considered the Underworld to be the source of disease, but also the source of healing. Shamans were people who knew how to travel to the Underworld and bring the healing back. "Modern show business is a direct response to [our] desire for a new healing therapy. Showbiz has grown out of the Shaman's healing magic... if you suffer from the Underworld, you can only be cured in the Underworld. It is a homeopathic principle...[Modern] show business hasgrown in importance because it provides just such a little dose of Underworld experience" (p.99).

that differs greatly from the theatre arts. Typically, mainstream actors know that they must appear at certain places and at certain times, with consequences if they do not. Traditional actors might very well experience performance burnout, but I doubt that they have ever even heard of burnout resulting from facilitation or actor support. It is, however, important to note that insufficient funding, a perpetual thorn for the small theatre company, likely played the largest role with respect to touring fatigue.

Critical Aspects of Performance, on the Road and at Home

Promotions

Promote, Promote, Promote!

If I have learned anything during my time with InsideOut, it is the value of promotions for theatre productions. Fundamentally, if there is no audience, there is no theatre, and without good promotion, the chances of securing a full house are negligible.[31] Where larger companies possess the resources necessary to finance hefty promotional initiatives, smaller companies like InsideOut cannot afford such luxuries. The solution, I discovered, was a team approach to promotions, relying heavily on word of mouth. The advent of email also opened new promotional opportunities for small companies but there is nothing like sharing the promotional burden of responsibility among all company members, their families, and support networks. Over the years, InsideOut Theatre has become a familiar interagency name within the community rehabilitation network in Calgary, Alberta. The theatre arts, slower to connect, have recently become aware of this specialised theatre company. The public, lags behind, and we continue to remain "the best-kept theatre secret in town". Our reputation has been earned through persistent and diligent

---

[31] It has often been said that InsideOut Theatre's best promotion is its show. I maintain that the arts can only be appreciated through personal experience, and this can occur as participation onstage, in rehearsal, or as an active audience member. Nevertheless, InsideOut has developed a number of promotional videos that have been invaluable to me when asked to guest lecture at an educational institution or conference. It is simply not always feasible to accommodate a performance, as ideal as this might be.

promotional efforts, and it is not outrageous to suggest that one day InsideOut Theatre will become a familiar name among the theatre-going public. Supports in the community, such as, the Calgary Alliance of Community Theatres (Calgary ACTS) and the Calgary Professional Arts Alliance (CPAA) are invaluable resources for spreading the word about a current production or training program. Flyers should be sent out at least twice before any production. People's lives are busy and complicated in these modern times. Potential audience members sometimes do not attend as they had planned. I find that, on average, one out of ten people who commit really do attend. For this reason, absolute belief in the entertainment value of the product is paramount. During the weeks leading up to a performance, the focus is clear, "Bums in Seats or Bust"! To reiterate: without an audience, there is no theatre. For the performers: the more energy coming from an audience, the better the show.[32]

The Audience

Audience is crucial to any theatre production, and generally, the larger the audience, the better the show. The artists with disabilities trust the experience they have with InsideOut Theatre both on and offstage. Onstage, the support and reassurance continues but, at times, it is also critical to choose the audience mindfully. Sometimes other class

---

[32] Some smaller theatre companies have been able to incorporate season tickets in their promotional packages, which can bolster ticket sales. InsideOut Theatre does not have a regular performance season, nor does a typical performance run more than two or three days. For these reasons, we have not been able to offer season tickets nor apply for government grants that require regular seasons or longer-running performance schedules. From the perspective of the smaller, innovative theatre company, a re-examination of funding criteria, as well as the definition of "professional theatre," would prove to be both innovative and refreshing.

participants will act as audience members (as in rehearsals). The level of performance will determine whether we present to an invited audience or to the general public. It is a matter of rapport. Taylor remarks on performances that "strongly hark back to the tribal intimacy of a nomadic show... [With] the strong rapport between performers and audience...The onlookers are purposively drawn into the action."[33] A work-in-progress performance, or the final show after a twelve-week basic training session would best be served by an audience consisting of friends, relatives, rehabilitation professionals, and others who have a grounded perspective about the challenges and rigours inherent in theatre training for actors with complex disabilities.

The general public can possess unrealistic notions of what is involved in a production of this nature. A curious paradox exists where public performances are concerned. On one hand, the public often arrives with minimal expectations of being entertained or moved in any way. Instead, however, they commonly experience gales of laughter and frequent moments of inspiration and delight. It is wonderful to hear audience members comment how watching our performance causes them to feel they too can perform! This is akin to underestimating how much time, energy, effort, creativity, and co-ordination goes into each and every performance.

InsideOut Theatre tests the edges of convention, as we exercise our right to be onstage. We promote cultural evolution by testing the boundaries of our audience members.[34] This is at the heart of the InsideOut Theatre dynamic. The development of the work is about expanding our cultural experience, ensuring that people with disabilities

---

[33] Taylor, p. 72.

[34] "The poems and songs that tell about adventures in the realms of spirits, the gestures, dances, and costumes, the art of communicating the extraordinary in all its many forms represent the very stuff of that which we now proudly designate as culture" (Taylor, p. 18).

are visible and that their voices are heard. When describing a healing séance, Taylor comments that the "magic is probably communicated through the Shaman's use of his (her) voice. The power of the spoken word [is] immensely potent."[35] InsideOut provides an opportunity for people with disabilities to have a voice and for audiences to listen.

As a group, an audience can be quite fickle. Each group of spectators takes on a psychology of its own. Predicting the responses of spectators to any given vignette is virtually impossible. Some crowds will laugh easily throughout the entire show, while others pick and choose bits and pieces with great irregularity. The closer an audience member is to the subject matter of any show, the more likely she or he is to connect with that performance. We can never know the full life experience of any one spectator, never mind an entire audience. Regardless, I would like to offer a hearty ovation to every audience member who has risked being educated by coming to an InsideOut production and, afterward, commending us with robust, heartfelt applause.

The advent of touring and the expanding phenomenon of Disability Theatre opened vistas of opportunities and challenges for InsideOut Theatre. The company's response to a growing obligation to its audience resulted in a focus on entertainment value while maintaining our authenticity as educators and advocates. The company continued to grow and take risks, and true to form, we took time to listen to all sides of any issue and then continued to do what worked for us. Something must have worked because politics and touring burnout aside, our shows continue to evoke gales of laughter and the inevitable catharsis that occurs when actor and audience connect.[36] There is nothing like a standing

---

[35] Taylor, p. 39.

[36] Taylor suggests that the religious aspect of Shamanism promoted a shared "exalted state of being" (p. 13). When there is a "strong rapport between performers and audiences... onlookers are purposefully drawn into the action, just as in the healing séance

ovation from an over-capacity crowd after an opening night performance. It is like a 'dream come true'.

---

some members would fall in with the Shaman's ecstasy" (p. 72). The lifting of the audience members' spirit is a "cure for the general human condition. Everybody is sick and [through performance], *everybody gets better*" (p. 41).

MILLENNIUM DREAMS

Introduction with sign language interpretation

Guitar playing theme song We Are Climbing the Ladder

Cast enters signing and singing.

Tableau

Millennium dreams

Harmony

Freedom

Television

Mischief

Growing up

Discover

Communication

Group

Happiness

Technology

Equality

Marriage

Prosperity

Reverence

Millennium Dreams

Voice: Live from Calgary, it's the Didi Show, and here is Didi Didi Didi!

Didi: We have a fabulous show for you this evening. We are here live in Calgary, Alberta, on the set of InsideOut, Calgary's finest integrated theatre company, and we are going to see their new show *Millennium Dreams*, and between the scenes we are going to interview the cast members. So I would like to introduce you to our first actor – Phil. Good afternoon, Phil.

Phil: Good afternoon.

Didi: Could you tell us a little bit about your disability?

Phil: Yes, I have a tendency to speak French all the time.

Didi: That must be so difficult for you. How do you cope?

Phil: Well, I decided to move to Calgary where French is appreciated.

Didi: Good idea.

Vignette 1

Jamie is watching a game show on TV.

Game Show Host: Welcome to "Who Wants To Get Rich Quick?." A, B, C, or D? Ummm D

Jamie: (saying to himself) I'm hungry and my sister is sleeping.

Goes next door.

Jamie: Hello, I'm Deaf and I don't know how to use the phone.

Neighbour: You don't know how to use a phone? Let me show you mine.

Jamie: My sister won't wake up, and I am hungry.

Neighbour: OK. First you have to phone Telus relay. Hi, Jamie here, can you phone 310 10 10?

Pizza Hut: Pizza Hut here.

Telus Relay: Hello, I have Jamie on the phone, and he would like to place an order.

Neighbour: Now type in your order. Hawaiian large.

Telus: Large Hawaiian

Pizza Hut: OK. Address?

Telus: Address please.

Neighbour: Type in your address. Make sure it is a large, and you better get the price.

Telus: Confirming address, size, and price.

Pizza Hut: The pizza will be $18.00.

Neighbour: OK. Confirm it and hang up.

Jamie: This is great. I've never seen this before.

Neighbour: They are expensive, but you really need to have one.

Jamie: Well, I am going to head back and wait for my pizza. Thanks for all the help.

Pays pizza deliveryman. Eats pizza.

Sister: Oh, you got pizza. How did you get that without my help?

End of vignette

Chanting: Didi, Didi, Didi.

Didi: Welcome back, and our next guest is Angela.

Didi: So Angela, why don't you tell the audience a little bit about your disability.

Angela: I am short.

Didi: How do you cope with it?

Angela: I have to work harder to buy clothes, and I have to suffer the smell down here.

Didi: I heard you have a very special guest in the audience today, would you like to say hello?

Angela: Hi, mom.

Didi: On with the show.

Vignette 2

Apart from the action on SR Angela sits writing a letter

Angela: I am writing you this letter to tell you that I have been reminiscing about our school days and how other children never used to include me in how they were playing.

CS action a soccer game commences

General Group: Soccer, soccer, but tall people only.

Captain 1 chooses a member.
Captain 2 chooses a member.
This continues.

Angela: I really want to play. I can play.

Adult: What is going on here?

Angela: They won't let me play because I am short.

Captain 2:   She is too short, and she could get hurt, and then whose responsibility is it?

Adult: Yours... And I have the ball. You can't play if you don't play with Angela.

Captain 2:   OK. Have you ever played before?

Angela: Yes

Captain 1:   We'll give you a five-point handicap because you took her on your team.

Game begins. Angela is given the ball. She immediately scores. General cheering.

Captain 2:   We want her on our team.

Captain 1:   No way, she is on our team.

Angela: (*highlighted and reading letter*) I hope you will come to Calgary and visit me soon and my new puppy, Tequila. Signing off, your friend, Angela.

End of vignette

Chanting: Didi, Didi, Didi.

Didi: We are back with InsideOut Theatre. Welcome now to Bob.

Didi: So Bob, you are definitely not short.

Bob: No.

Didi: Could you talk a little about your disability?

Bob: My disability is hard to talk about. It starts with the B word.

Didi: Well there is more appropriate terminology for your disability now.

Bob: It's called follically challenged.

Didi: So *bald*, I mean, *Bob*. So, how do you cope with your disability?

Bob: Hats, lots of hats.

Vignette 3

Ruth: Are we going to get a coffee break today or what?

Bob: Well, we have thirty clients and two hours.

Ruth: Dressed or undressed?

Factory procedure: OK. Wash up, open up, eat your porridge, keep moving, wake up. Take your meds, yes, you two. Eat your breakfast. Open up, keep going.

Bell rings.

Ruth: Coffee break.

Gang takes a coffee break. One support person stays behind to visit and help clients.

Ruth: Make her stop that. She is making us look bad.

Bob: I'll stop her.

Pam: Yeah, just feed and clean them, don't talk to them.

Angela: But I enjoy speaking to them.

Bob: If you want to be part of our team, you'll stop that now.

Angela: OK.

End of vignette

Didi: And now we are going to visit with Pamela.

Pam: Hello.

Didi: What is your disability?

Pam: Cheekbones.

Didi: Cheekbones?

Pam?   Everyone looks at my cheekbones, they want them, and they admire them.

Didi: You seem a bit angry. A bit of a chip on your shoulder.

Pam: I do not. I have learned to cope. What are you saying?

Didi: Let's give Pam a hand.

Vignette 4

Class: Big test today.

Nicky: Did you study?,,,, oh there she is.

Teacher: Silence. I have math tests here, and I am going to put them face down on the desk. Oh, I have someone with a learning disability here who needs extra time. (*To student with obvious physical disability*) Oh, you poor sweet boy, you can have all the time that you need. No questions, put your hands down. This test is worth 50% of your year's mark.

Pencils ready!

Nicky keeps putting up her hand.

Teacher: 3, 2, 1 go!

Teacher paces and shouts at the kids.

Teacher: (*to child she thinks has disability*) You take your time, dear.

Phil: I am done.

Teacher: No, you are not, you have a disability.

Phil: But I'm done.

Teacher: This is a miracle, disabled person finished. 3, 2, 1 STOP!

Teacher: Look at Phil; he obviously has the disability. Big strong girl like you obviously doesn't have a disability!

Nicky: Check the name.

Teacher: Oh, oh, my gosh I, I guess you are right. Well, keep working, Nicky.

Nicky: Listen, Phil may be smart, but I am smart too, I am just slow.

Teacher: Well, you are smart, and I am hungry. And since you are so smart, you take the time that you need, and when you are done place your paper on my desk. Can you do that?

Nicky continues to work, then places the test on the desk.

End of vignette

Chanting for Didi.

Didi: Next we are going to talk to Robert. Hello Robert.

Robert: Hello.

Didi: Now could you tell us a little bit about your disability?

Robert: I don't have a disability.

Didi: No?

Robert: No.

Didi: Well, they said it was an integrated theatre company. Thanks, Robert.

Vignette 5

Everyone chatting.

Voice over: (*news program*) Shortfalls are threatening revenues for people with disabilities. Mayor is not unsympathetic to people's situations, but he wants this carefully examined.

PwD 1: What are we going to do? (*PwD stands for Person with a Disability.*)

PwD 2: I don't know. What can we do?

PwD 3: What are we going to do?

PwD2: I tried the drop-in centre, but they are full.

PwD 1: Let's go ask for some money. We'll go together.

Everyone starts to ask the audience for money.

PwD1: Fifty bucks, I got fifty bucks.

Sound of police sirens.

Cop: All right, we have had a complaint about unlawful soliciting.

PwD 1: We have nowhere to stay, our financial support has been cut.

Cop: No place to stay? I've got a place for you to stay.

PwD 2: Great.

Cop: Yeah, downtown in jail.

PwD 1: I have a rich uncle; maybe we could go and stay with him.

Knock, knock.

Uncle: Who are you?

PwD 1: I am your niece Helen.

Aunt: Oh, hello Helen. Who are these guys?

Helen: My husband and friend.

Aunt: Well, come on in for a cup of coffee.

They enter a teeny, tiny apartment.

Aunt: It is so very nice to see you.

Uncle: Do you want a cigar?

Aunt: So how long are you staying?

Helen: Indefinitely.

Aunt/Uncle: Indefinitely. Ooooohhh nooooo.

End of vignette

Intermission

Introduction to second half

Group recites poem: We are special people. We are
equal and the same.
Families were divided, which was a shame, we were meant
to be together. We are equal and the same.
Segregation was for children; they were not free to play; we
are not different. We are equal and the same.
Then there was sterilisation; the government was to blame;
we are loved and we love. We are equal and the same.
Today we have a future, to be part of the game; we are
strong.

We are equal and the same.
For now we look ahead hoping for some fame; magical
moments encircle us; the light of life is in us all. We are
equal and the same.

Crowd chants, Didi.Didi. Didi.

Didi: OK. We are back and just to kick this off, we are

going to talk to the director of InsideOut Theatre, Ruth Bieber. Hey, Ruth, how are you?

Ruth: I am well, thank you.

Didi: Tell us a bit about your disability.

Ruth: Well, it first started in junior high.

Didi: Oh, so you weren't born with it?

Ruth: No, it was developmental.

Didi: Oh, I've heard about that before. Do you feel comfortable talking about it?

Ruth: Well, it's every young girl's nightmare to be in junior high and to be flat chested.

Didi: Oooooh, that is terrible. How do you cope?

Ruth: Well, for years and years I put my faith in falsies. Sorry, false hope. And then I got pregnant and thought things would flesh out, but things fell flat. But I have decided that, as a woman, I am more than a set of breasts, and ever since, then things have been perky in my life.

Didi: That is a wonderful story, Ruth! Let us hear it for the director of InsideOut.

Vignette 6

Mother: Oh my goodness, what a day I have had as a working mother. How are you, dear?

Husband: Fine

Mother: How is it going, Grandma?

Grandma: Fine, I am making chilli for supper.

Mother: Oh, that's great. I am just fried. Can I try? Oooh, spicy, like you!

Daughter 1 (Connie):   Mom, Mom I just got an honour's on the report card.

Mother: Well, of course you did, but that does not excuse you from cleaning your room.

Connie: But Mom.

Mother: But nothing. I don't need this attitude from you. You are in need of an attitude adjustment, young lady. Off to your room now.

Connie stomps off.

Daughter 2 (Angela):   Mom, Dad, I got an A+ on my report card.

Mother: Oh, Angela, you have worked so hard. And a birthday invitation. We are so proud of you.

Grandma: And I have a puppy for you for being such a wonderful child.

Phone rings.

Mother: Hello.

Teacher: Hello, I am phoning from the school where Angela and Connie go.

Mother: What's the problem?

Teacher: Well, Connie has been having some problems at school these days.

Mother: But she is an honour roll student.

Teacher: Yes, but I feel that she is not getting the attention she needs at home, so she is acting out at school.

Mother: She gets plenty of attention at home.

Teacher: Well, we don't mean that kind of attention. She needs the kind of positive attention you give to Angela.

Mother: But I thought she was doing so well. And Angela has always been the one with all the special needs and appointments that we just really have focused on that, and what with Connie doing so well in school.

Teacher: I hope you can give some honest thought to this feedback and maybe spend some more time with Connie and her needs.

Mother puts down the phone and looks toward father.

Mother: That was the teacher from the school, and she wants to talk to us about Connie next week. She thinks we don't pay attention to Connie enough. She thinks that both our daughters require the same amount of attention. What do you think?

Father: I agree.

Mother: I have an idea, we'll go out for supper and have a family conference, and we'll make changes that work for us all. And…Grandma got her pension cheque, she can pay for dinner. Come on girls, get your coats.

Connie: What?

Mother: We are going out for supper for a family conference, but don't worry, I think you are going to like what I am going to say. We are going to make some changes around here.

Grandma: Where is everyone going?

Mother: Can't forget Grandma 'cause she is buying.

End of vignette

Chanting: Didi Didi Didi Didi

Didi: I am now going to introduce a long-time member of the InsideOut Theatre Company, Helen. Hello, Helen.

Helen: Hello, Didi.

Didi: How long have you been with the company?

Helen: Ten years.

Didi: What is your disability?

Helen: I grew up.

Didi: That is terrible.

Helen: It started when I was two and just keeps happening.

Didi: Well, you seem to be coping well.

Vignette 7

Workers.

Pam: How about those Flames, Bob?

Bob: What Flames?

Pam: How about you, Phil?

Phil: Not interested.

Pam: Here's the boss.

Boss: Get making the donuts.

Pam: I thought you were only going to be here for a short time, but it's been six months already.

Bob: How long have you been here?

Pam: Eighteen.

Bob: The floor here sure is dirty.

Pam: Yeah, it's never clean.

Boss: I've been advertising for months for some extra help to try and keep it clean.

Pam: Yeah, and there are eggshells and garbage back here that are really smelly.

Boss: Yeah, I know. Hope the food inspectors don't show up.

Knock, knock, knock.

Person: I've come about the job you've advertised for someone to clean the floor.

Boss: Well, have you got some experience?

Person: Well, I have a disability, so I haven't really got a lot of employment experience yet.

Boss: How hard can it be to use a broom? Go for it and try it.

Person begins sweeping. Starts to get into trouble. Is doing everything wrong.

Boss: This is a disaster.

Pam: Disabled person, ya know. One of those. More trouble.

Boss: I'm sorry but we have Workers' Compensation to worry about so you just won't cut it.

Ten Years Later

Bob: I thought this was a temporary position.

Pam: Time flies.

Boss: Morning crew, how are ya doing? Orders for sixty dozen donuts, get to work.

Pam: Good thing we are fully automated, but the floor is still dirty. Someone could fall and slip.

Boss: I'm still posting the advertisement for the job.

Person with a Disability (PwD): I saw the ad in the paper and, I am applying for the job.

Boss: Who are you?

Support person: Her support partner. I help her out if she needs it.

Boss: Really sounds good. Go for it.

The two of them clean the floor efficiently. Everyone is happy.

Pam: Can you do the garbage and eggshells too? Can you come everyday?

PwD: No problem.

Pam: Hey, who knew the floor was green?

Bob: This person is great.

Pam: She's got my vote.

Boss: Was she in the way?

Gang: No way, we want her. See ya tomorrow. Keep up the good work.

Boss: I don't have to pay both of you, do I?

Support Person: No.

Boss: Technology is great, but people power is better.

End of vignette

Audience chanting for Didi.

Didi: Next we are going to talk to Connie. Hello, Connie.

Connie: Hello, Didi.

Didi: Can you tell me a little bit about your disability?

Connie: It's quite sad, I have artistic personality disorder.

Didi: Oh, that sounds awful. Do you treat it with medication?

Connie: No, no, I just cope.

Didi: Is it dangerous?

Connie: Well, it can be. I leave my art supplies all over the place, and I am constantly tripping on them, and I have these dramatic mood impulses.

Didi: I am so very sorry. How do you cope?

Connie: Well, I found a theatre group called InsideOut, and they understand what I am going through, and they let my artistic personality unleash on the stage.

Didi: Well good for you. I am glad you found such a creative outlet.

Vignette 8

Pastor: Well, here we are at the Centre of Faith, Hope, and Charity. I am the director, and I have many appointments.

(*This is a repeat vignette, now contextualised for the "Didi Show."*)

Knocking.

Pastor: Hello, come in.

Connie: I'm Connie.

Henry: And I'm Henry.

Pastor: What can I do for you two young people today?

Connie: We are here for your pre-marriage seminar.

Pastor: We are so well known for them. What do you want to know?

Connie: Well, we want to sign up.

Pastor: For heaven's sake, why?

Connie: Well, we are getting married.

Pastor: You have disabilities.

Connie: But they are no big deal.

Pastor: Well, they may be no big deal to you, but I am afraid I am going to need the signatures of your legal guardians before we can consider this at all.

Connie: But we are our own legal guardians.

Pastor: What? Perhaps you think you are, but I doubt it, and I would like to speak to your parents. I have to answer to my parishioners.

Henry: Let's get our parents.

Pastor: Impossible.

Knocking.

Pastor: Well that was fast.

Connie: This is my mother and Henry's father.

Mother: Hello.

Father: Hello.

Pastor: Hello, so kind of you to come today. I understand that your children wish to marry.

Mother: Of course, they want to.

Pastor: Of course, so you know?

Mother: Yes.

Pastor: Really? And how do you feel about this?

Mother: We are happy of course.

Pastor: Happy?

Mother: Yes.

Pastor: Well, you know that you must realize that marriage is a very big commitment.

Connie: We've been living together for years.

Pastor: You need a job.

Connie: I've been working for five years and Henry for seven.

Pastor: Really. So you are employed. But you must live with your parents.

Connie: No, we have our own apartment.

Pastor: But you visit?

Connie: Almost never.

Pastor: But I need the signature.

Connie: You need our signatures, not our parents'.

Mother: I think you have a bit of a sheltered life here. I am a lawyer, and these people are their own legal guardians and are entitled to be married.

Pastor: Well, then I guess I had better give you the agenda for the sessions. We start with communications, then finances, and human sexuality.

Connie: Oh, we really want to take that class.

Pastor: What for? You are not planning on having children are you?

Connie: Well, we want children.

Mother: We would love grandchildren. We are happy about this.

Pastor: Happy, happy, everybody is happy about this? Oh, for goodness sake, I'll see you in class on Tuesday.

End of vignette

Chanting for Didi Didi Didi Didi Didi Didi Didi Didi Didi Didi.

Didi: And now I would like to interview another member of the company, Ms. Selma.

Selma: *Signs, "Hello."*

Didi: Would you mind discussing your disability with us, Selma?

Selma: My vision requires that I wear glasses.

Didi: Well, I wear glasses, and I never thought of it as a disability.

Selma: I think you might be living in a certain denial.

Didi: Really. And how do you cope?

Selma: I take it day by day, get out of bed, and start again. Listen to the taunts of "four eyes!" But I have found buying dozens of pairs of glasses in different styles and colours has helped. Now I get new names. Cool chick. Sophisticated lady.

Didi: Well thank you for that advice, Selma

Vignette 9

Phil: As you should know, Mom, I am moving out.

Mom: Moving out!

Phil: I am getting older and feel like I should move out.

Mom: This is your home. I take care of you.

Phil: I have already decided, and I have placed an ad in the newspaper for a roommate, and I am interviewing three different applicants today.

Mom: Today!

Knocking at door.

Phil: Hello.

Person 1:   Hi. I'm here about the ad. Can you pay me $500.00 bucks a month?

Phil: No, I can only do $250.00.

Person 1:   Do you have any more?

Phil: No, I am poor.

Person 1:   Do you have a colour TV?

Phil: No, just a black and white one.

Person 1:   Got a microwave?

Phil: No, I don't believe in microwaves.

Mom: Phil, I don't think this is the right roommate for you. He just wants your money and stuff.

Phil: You're right. Get out of here.

Mom: You are not going to find anyone. You should stay here. The world is not safe.

Knocking.

Phil: I'll get it. Come in.

Couple: Oh, you poor boy. Don't you worry, we'll look after you. We are from the Agency called Tender Loving Care. We've got ramps, we've got beds, we can feed you, and we can dress you.

Phil: Are you psycho?

Couple: No, we are just full of love; we'll look after you. We require your doctor's phone number, all your medications, all your assistance from homecare, and would you like to write us a cheque now or later?

Phil: I've changed my mind.

Couple: No, we can look after you.

Mom: Phil, these people are terrible. They just want to take care of you. My son doesn't require this kind of care. He is an independent young man.

Phil: You are right. Get out.

Couple: We are definitely unappreciated here.

Mom: This is hard. How will you ever find anyone?

Knocking.

Person 3:   Are you looking for a roommate cause I have an apartment, and the rent is $500.00 and I thought we could split?

Phil: That would work for my budget.

Person 3:   That's OK. Can you cook?

Phil: Yes, but I burn stuff a lot and it smells.

Person 3:   We can work around that. But I am at work all day. Can you cope on your own?

Phil: Oh, yes.

Person 3:   Well, the apartment is only six blocks from here, so why don't you come and take a look?

Phil: Great!

Mom: Phil? Couldn't I come too?

Person 3:   Sure, we'll walk slowly.

End of vignette

Audience chanting for Didi.

Didi: We are now going to talk to another veteran of InsideOut Theatre, Billy.

Didi: Hello, Billy.

Billy: Hello.

Didi: How long have you been with the company?

Billy: Six years.

Didi: Can you tell us a little bit about your disability?

Billy: No.

Didi: OK.

Vignette 10

Tom: Just because you are my guardian doesn't make you the boss of me. I am going to move out with my girlfriend and take care of myself.

Guardian: No way, you have no job, and you don't know how to take care of yourself.

Tom: I am moving in with my girlfriend, and you can't boss me.

Guardian exits and Helen enters

Tom: He is always telling me what to eat, when to sleep, how to spend my money.

Helen: You got to get out of there.

Tom: Are you your own guardian?

Helen: Yes, I am.

Tom: I would like that. Can you tell me how to do that?

And by the way could you buy me a coffee.

Helen: Sure, let's go, and get this in the works.

End of vignette

Audience for Didi.

Didi: Hello, and what is your name?

Jamie: Jamie, and my disability is that I am way too nice.

Didi: I don't know what to say.

Jamie: When I write I always use dear, sincerely, thank you, please.

Didi: That is so sad, how do you cope?

Jamie: You just use your brain.

Didi: Sounds like a good solution to me.

Vignette 11

Jamie: Well, I finally got my Telus instant relay, and I found an affordable one.

Selma: Hey Jamie, how are you?

Jamie: Time flies. I have something to show you. See, I got my own TTY.

Selma: Finally.

Jamie: Yeah, and it's portable, so I can take it everywhere.

Selma: Pretty fancy.

Jamie: Yep, I am just waiting for my first call.

Phone rings.

Jamie: Hey, look!

Telus Relay: Hello, I am a Belgian producer looking for Steven Spielberg.

Jamie: This is Jamie on the line. Are you calling from Hollywood?

Telus: Yes, I am looking for Steven Spielberg.

Jamie: My first number is a wrong number.

Selma: Your first call was long distance.

Selma: Well, I am going to go home, why don't you call me?

Jamie: I will. I just love technology like this.

THE END

HELP UNWANTED

Opening – group moves onstage singing and signing the words to the InsideOut theme song.

Group: We are climbing the ladder to a better way, we are fighting each day for our rights, everyone stand up and shout, We Are InsideOut.

Sung twice.

Tableau and Theme Scene

One person crouches and says "Help."

Each successive person attaches himself or herself in a physical way to the next person and shouts out a word that represents, to them, Help Unwanted.

When everyone is in a frozen physical pose, they say in unison "Help unwanted."!

From offstage enters a Helpful Bystander (HB) who is shocked to see the group.

HB: Oh, look at all these people with disabilities. They must need my help. Excuse me, can I help you?

The tableau breaks apart as actors run screaming in fear offstage, and away from Helpful Bystander. Only one member of the group remains.

HB: (*sees a person with a disability left on the stage asks him*) Do you want any help?

Person: I just want to watch TV.

HB: OK. Let's go.

They exit the stage.

Music cue

CHORUS

Hidey Hidey Hidey Hidey Hidey Hidey Hey
You like to keep us busy
To keep us on the run.
Bowling, Swimming, Working, too
And having LOTS of fun.
But sometimes we're just lazy,
And TV is our friend.
So let us gaze into the haze,
We'll love you to the end.
Oooooooohhhh.

Vignette 1

Person 1 enters, goes centre stage (CS) and sits in a chair staring straight ahead.

Support 1:   (*enters talking*) Oh, goodness! Are you STILL sitting here watching TV? You know that you are supposed to be going to your work placement! Your daytime support is going to be here any minute, and do you know who they are going to blame? Me! You are making me crazy…and…what are you watching? Oh, it's the final episode of "Normality Sucks." I love this show.

Support 2:   (*enters*) What is going on here? Why isn't he (or she) ready for work? What have you been doing? You know how important this work placement is for him and how difficult it was to get? What are you two watching? Goodness, "Normality Sucks." Is this the final episode?

Girlfriend: (*enters*) You know, I have been waiting for you to call and you haven't. You are my boyfriend, and that means you are supposed to call and we are supposed to go out. Oh, my goodness, it's "Normality Sucks."

Enter parent who walks in front of the TV and is yelled at to move.

Parent: What are you guys doing? Is nobody helping her (or him) to get ready for work?

Support 1:   But, but, it's "Normality Sucks!"

Parent: What. Oh,wow! Is she going to eat that spider?

Support 1:   She is such a bitch.

Support 2:   We hate her.

Parent: Whoa, whoa, whoa. He/She still has to get to work. Now get up, come on, get ready.

Everyone pushes Person 1 off the chair and out, then they all scramble towards the chair and sit all over each other.

Everyone: (*in unison*) We just want to watch TV.

Music cue

End of vignette.

CHORUS

Ooohhhh, hidey, hidey, hidey hidey hidey hidey hey
We like a little romance.
We like to mess around.

But when the crisis happen,
Don't push us to the ground.
We're trying to tell you something
Through all this squawky sound.
But just be loose and patient,
And meaning will abound.
Ooooooooooohhhhh hidey hidey hidey hidey hidey hidey hey!

Vignette 2

Secretary: (*Sitting onstage with keyboard in her lap, typing away. She hits a bell and yells.*) Next!

Offstage scream.

Enter woman in labour and her husband.

Pregnant Woman: Ohhhhhhhhhhhh, pant, pant pant.

Husband: Breathe, breathe.

Secretary: Health Care number, home phone, address?

Pregnant Woman: Aaaarrrgghhh, it hurts!!!!

Husband: Breathe, you can do it.

Secretary: Nurse!

Nurse enters.

Nurse: Really, I was just going on coffee and... oh, my goodness, you poor man, you are out of control. (*runs and tries to assist the husband*) Just give me some focus; I'm your friend. I can help.

Husband: Breathe, oh please, breathe.

Nurse: Doctor!

Doctor: Yes, what seems to be… oh, my goodness. Don't worry, I'm here to help.

Nurse: I think he belongs on the seventh floor. (*motions with her hand that he is crazy*)

Doctor: I think you're right. Come along, buddy, we are here to help you.

Husband: Breathe, breathe.

Nurse: Yes, breathing is good.

The doctor and nurse guide the husband in front of the secretary and wife, who at that moment, triumphantly delivers a baby.

Husband: It's a boy! It's a boy!

Nurse: Yes, you are a good boy, now come along with us.

Doctor, nurse, and husband exit.

Secretary: Security!!!

Enter Security.

Security: Yes, what do we have. Oh, my! You sure have made a mess here.

Wife: Have you any scissors?

Security: Scissors? Around a baby? Are you crazy? You better come with me.

Wife and Security exit.

Secretary: (*hits bell, yells*) Next.

Music cue

End of vignette

CHORUS

Oooooooh Hidey hidey hidey hidey hidey hidey hey
If bathing is your forte,
If shampoo makes you squeal,
If soapy water and naked skin
Excites you like a seal,
We've got a paraplegic,
For your own heart's appeal,
But if he says, "Enough's enough."
Please get real!

Vignette 3

Enter Bather with towel and underwear and magazine. Bather gets into the tub.

Bather: Ah, there is nothing like a great, long, hot bath. I am going to lie in here all morning. Just my magazine, my rubber ducky, and me. This is the life.

Enter three support partners and another person with a disability wrapped in a towel.

Support 1:   (*To bather*) What in the world are you doing in here?

Bather: Aaarrgh. Get out, this is my time.

Support 1:   Your time. What are you talking about? Who is supposed to bathing at 4:00?

Support 2:   (*looks at clipboard*) Ah, that would be Dustin.

Support 1:   You don't look like Dustin. You look like Phil, and this is not Phil's bath time. When is Phil's bath time?

Support 2:   7:00.

Support 1:   And it's not 7:00 o'clock. That's queue jumping. Mark that down.

Support 2:   Marked.

Support 1:   Well, let's get him out.

Support 3:   Hey guys, it's almost our break time, and he's already in there.

Support 1:   So?

Support 3:   So, let's clean him up, and then we don't have to bathe him later. We can grab an extra break.

Support 1:   Good thinking. OK. Aaahh, what kind of shampoo is he authorized to use?

Support 2:   (*checking clipboard*) Baby shampoo.

Support 1:   You know why, don't you? Cause you won't

close your eyes when we rinse your hair. (*continues to scrub*) Can you check with the doctor and see if we can use some dandruff shampoo? He has a lot of flakes.

Bather: I do not!

Support 1:   Close your eyes. You never listen.

Support 2:   OK. Time to get you out of here. On three let's lift him. 1-2-

Bather makes huge farting noises.

Support 1:   Oh, that is so gross. You do that on purpose, you know.

Support 2:   It's why you have no friends.

Support 1:   What did he have for lunch?

Support 3:   (*checking list*) Cabbage rolls and beans.

Support 1:   Make a note to the nutritionist that he should be put on a clear broth diet.

Support 3:   Noted.

Support 1:   OK. You are so out of here. 1, 2, 3

They lift the bather out of the tub.

Support 3:   (*picking up a pair of underwear*) Hey, what's with this?

Bather: It's nothing, just the remains of a little wet dream.

Support drops the underwear.

Support 1:   Mark that down. He's exhibiting delusional behaviour. Now, you know you don't have wet dreams. People like you don't. What you have are accidents. Make a note that he needs some adult Depends.

Support 3:   Noted.

Support 1:   (*to other person with a disability, who has been watching the support partners and enjoying the bather's attitude*) OK. Now let's get you ready.

Support 2:   Ahem, aaah. You know, it's getting pretty late for our break, and I could really use a smoke.

Support 1:   Oh, yeah, well ahhh. How about ... Hey, why don't these two guys hang out for a while? Get to know each other and socialise a bit. We'll go for a quick coffee and be back in 15.

Support 2:   30.

Support 3:   45 minutes, tops.

Support 1:   Yeah, and don't go into the bathtub. Liability and all. OK. Get to know each other, guys.

Exit the support partners.

Bather: Don't pay any attention to those guys, they are totally crazy. Hey, let's go and watch TV completely naked.

Music cue.

End of vignette

CHORUS

Oooooooooohhhhh hidey hidey hidey hidey hidey hidey hey
You think your job's important.
You think you're quite a hit.
But when we come in snorting,
Don't make us pitch a fit.
We're trying to tell you something,
This ain't no time for wit.
And when the joking's over,
Well, hey, you know that's it.
Ooooooooohhhhhhh hidey hidey hidey hidey hidey hidey
hey

Vignette 4

Secretary seated CS, typing on her keyboard.

Secretary: (*rings bell, yells*) Next!!

*Offstage, loud choking and gagging sounds. Enter husband
and wife.*

Husband: Breathe, what's the matter? Breathe.

Wife, choking and grabbing her throat.

Secretary: Health Care number. Address. Phone
number.

Wife falls to the floor, dead.

Husband starts screaming.

Secretary: Nurse.

Nurse: Really, always on my break. Oh, my goodness, it's you again. Look at me, this is important. I'm your friend. Doctor!!!

Doctor: Is this important because ... oh it's him.

Nurse: He's hysterical this time. I can't make any sense of what he's saying.

Doctor: He obviously needs medical attention. I just happen to have something that will fix him right up.

Reaches into his pocket and pulls out a syringe and injects it.

Husband: (*all woozy*) That feels groovy man. (*He passes out.*)

Nurse: (*checks his pulse and notices his wrist*) Wow, that worked fast. What did you give him?

Doctor: Morphine. It's the best.

Nurse: His Medic Alert bracelet says he has anaphylaxis to morphine...I wasn't here. I cannot have been here.

Nurse exits.

Doctor: Anaphylaxis?

Secretary: It's a life-threatening allergic condition.

Doctor: I knew that. Well, he should have said something.

Doctor runs offstage.

Secretary: Security!!

Security enters.

Security: Two dead bodies today?

Secretary: Just doing my job.

Security: Well, I will take one now and come back for the other after coffee.

Security drags one offstage.

Secretary: (*hits the bell, yells*) Next!

Music cue.

End of vignette

CHORUS

Ooooooooooohhhhh hidey hidey hidey hidey hidey hidey hey
You're feeling kinda plucky,
And, oh by George, what luck.
Not one, not two, not three,
It's a gold mine you have struck!
You want to be a hero,
But the words just run amuck.
They cross the street without your help,

And you're flattened by a truck.
Ooooooooooohhhhh hidey hidey hidey hidey hidey hidey hey

Vignette 5

Person 1:   Hey, how ya doing?

Person 2:   Great, just got myself a new job.

Person 1:   Wow, good news, got time for a drink?

Person 2:   Just 15 minutes. I'm on my coffee break.

Person 1:   There is a pub across the street, let's go.

Enter a person with a disability (PwD), either in wheelchair or having difficulty with mobility.

Person 2:   Oh, oh, oh, look over there.

Person 1:   What? Oh, that's so sad.

Person 2:   I saw this program on cable.

Person 1:   You watch cable?

Person 2:   Hey, I was unemployed!

Person 1:   Oh, yeah.

Person 2:   Anyways, the program said, "Just ask if they need assistance."

Person 1:   So?

Person 2:   So go and ask if he needs assistance.

Person 1:   Me? I didn't see this program.

Person 2:   I have total faith in you. Go be a good citizen.

Person 1:   OK.

Walks over to PwD.

Person 1:   Do you need any help walking across the …

Person 2 drags Person 1 back.

Person 2:   What are you saying? Look at this guy. Does he look like he can walk?

Person 1:   Not well.

Person 2:   Well, then don't say "walk." You've probably made him angry.

Person 1:   He doesn't look happy.

Person 2:   Listen, try again, you mean well. Just don't say "Walk."

Person 1:   OK. I got it. Ahem. Do you need some help … hobbling across the street?

Person 2:   (*dragging Person 1 back again*) What are you saying? Hobbling?

Person 1:   Well, that's what he does.

Person 2:   We all do things we don't talk about. Now you've made him real mad.

Person 1:   What should I do?

Person 2:   Go set it right, and for goodness sake don't say "Hobble."

Person 1:   Umm, do you need any help … getting

across the street?

PwD 1:   NO!

PwD 1 crosses the street by himself.

Person 1:   He said No!

Person 2:   How rude.

Person 1:   And we missed the light.

Person 2:   Look, look, look.

Enter PwD 2 and 3 (both Deaf). They are signing a conversation about life, boyfriends, etc.

Person 1:   No way, I'm not doing it.

Person 2:   This is your chance to redeem yourself. I have faith in you.

Person 1:   I don't have faith in myself.

Person 2:   Breathe. Centre.

Person 1:   Meditation stance. Auuuuummmmmmmmm

Person 2:   Go!

Person 2:   Excuse me, excuse me.

People who are Deaf look confused. Sign to her that they can't hear.

Person 2:   (*speaking to Person 1*) Maybe I should

speak louder? HELLO! (*screams in Deaf couple's ears.*)

Deaf couple look offended. Signing to each other about her rudeness.

Person 2:   (*to Person 1*) Hey, I know. I took these drama classes. I can just act out what I want to say.

Person 2:   (*doing big body movements, pointing at the two*) You two need help! Oh, yeah. SOS. (*begins doing big semaphore movements and whacks one person who is Deaf on the back of the head*)

Deaf couple are totally annoyed. They stomp off, signing to each other that she is an idiot.

Person 2:   Did you see that?

Person 1:   They were really annoyed with you.

Person 2:   So rude. Next time they need help, I am not going to help them. Then they'll be sorry.

Person 1:   And we missed the green light, again!

Person 2:   These disabled people are ruining our coffee break.

Enter a person who is blind.

Person 1:   (*extremely excited*) Oh, my goodness! Look! It's your lucky day!

Person 2:   (*exasperated*) Oh no, not me. No way.

Person 1:   You've had two strikes. Now is your time for

redemption, time for a home run.

Person 2:   You do it then.

Person 1:   This is your moment. You can do this.

Person 2:   (*sobbing*) I can't.

Person 1:   Get in there slugger. But don't blow it. Just ask him if he needs assistance.

Person 2:   OK. (*sniffling*)

Person 2:   Nice weather we're having?

Person 1:   No, no, no, no. Get back here.

Person 2:   What?

Person 1:   He is blind. He cannot see the weather. Don't talk about the weather. You are going to make him angry. Just ask him if he needs assistance.

Person 2:   Oh, OK.

Person 2:   Do you need any help getting across the street?

Blind person: No.

Sound cue: ding ding ding ding ding ding.

Person who is blind crosses the street.

Two people are looking up and around trying to understand the sound.

Person 1:   Is there a truck backing up?

Person 2:   I thought that was the seatbelt-fasten signal.

Person 1:   I get it. That's a sound cue to let blind people know when to cross the street.

Person 2:   He still should have taken my help.

Person 1:   And we missed the green light. AGAIN!!!

Person 2:   I know. Let's jaywalk.

Person 1:   On the count of three. One ... two... three...

Sound cue: screeching tires and smashing metal.

Blackout.

Music cue

End of vignette

CHORUS

Oooooooooohhhhh hidey hidey hidey hidey hidey hidey hey
If shopping is your passion,
You'd better choose a lane.
You'll suddenly turn a corner,
There'll be someone with a cane.
You'll start to feel real nosy
You might even go insane.
But don't be feeling guilty,
Cause it turns out YOU'RE the pain.
Oooooooooohhhhh hidey hidey hidey hidey hidey hidey hey

Vignette 6

A group of people is in line at the checkout counter. One person is the cashier, with an assistant bagging. One person in the line has an obvious disability (PwD). Behind that person are two people who are together, Sisters 1 and 2. Behind them is another shopper.

Sister 1:   For crying out loud, we ALWAYS get the slow line behind one of THESE people. They take forever.

Sister 2:   Well, they move slower, and we don't have anywhere to go anyhow.

Sister 1:   That is not the point.

PwD coughs.

Sister 1:   Eeewwww gross. Good Grief, he just went spreading his group home germs all over the place. These people have loads of viruses because they don't understand about hygiene. Good Grief. We are going to have to wash all of our fruit as soon as we get home.

Sister 2 offers the person a Kleenex, much to her sister's annoyance.

Sister 1:   *(peering over the grocery cart of the person with a disability)* Oh, My Heavens! This is rich. Get this, the guy is buying… condoms. Hilarious.

Sister 2:   What's so funny? He probably is planning on having sex.

Sister 1:   Don't be sick. People like him don't have sex. Yuck, don't even talk about it. He is probably going to make balloon animals with them.

Cashier: Will that be cash?

PwD: I'm sorry, I don't have any cash.

Sister 1:   Classic! No cash.

Sister 2:   We could loan him some.

Sister 1:   Stop it!

PwD: But I could put it on my Gold Credit Card.

Cashier: That'll do.

Sister 1:   Gold Credit Card. WE can't get a Gold Credit Card. What is he... Ooooh, I get it. He's probably getting a monthly allowance. These guys get thousands of bucks a month just to be disabled, and then they take that money and stockpile it in the Cayman Islands. That's taxpayer's money he's spending, that's my money!

Sister 2:   We don't pay taxes.

Sister 1:   That is not the point.

Cashier: Sign here, please.

Sister 1:   (*to PwD*) It ain't an epic novel.

Sister 2:   Take your time, sonny.

Cashier: Next.

Sister 1:   Could you move it, we've been in line all day.

Cashier: Yeah, sure, but first let's get something

straight. Who is paying?

Sister 1 and 2:   (*in unison*) She is!

Sister 1:   I can't pay. I need my money for cigarettes.

Sister 2:   Well, I paid for Bingo, and it's not my turn.

Sister 1:   Is too.

Sister 2:   Is not.

Cashier: Can we get a stockperson to till 4? The Baldwin sisters cannot pay. AGAIN.

Sister 1:   How rude. I don't have to take this. I can shop elsewhere.

Cashier: Suit yourself.

Sister 2:   Don't mind my sister. She hasn't had sex in a month.

Cashier: Too much information.

Music cue: elevator music as everyone waits for the stock person.

Cashier: (*to next person in line*) Sorry, ma'am. (*or sir*) They seem a bit slow on the floor, you'll have to go to another line.

Shopper: (*huge sigh*) Fine, but I haven't had sex in years!!

Music cue

End of Vignette

CHORUS

Ooooooooooohhhhh hidey hidey hidey hidey hidey hidey hey
We like to live together.
We like to live alone.
Don't put us on a tether.
It'll only make us groan.
But, when we're feeling nervous--Cause the situation's new,
Don't leave us unsupported
Or we might move in with YOU.
Ooooooooooohhhhh hidey hidey hidey hidey hidey hidey hey

Vignette 7

Mother and Daughter onstage facing away from each other. Daughter wearing a bathrobe and holding a bag of chips. Phone rings.

Daughter: Hello, Mother.

Mother: How did you know it was me, darling?

Daughter: It's ALWAYS you, Mother.

Mother: Well, a little enthusiasm would be nice. I have some wonderful and exciting news for you, but business before pleasure. I've got the checklist ready, darling.

Daughter: Yes, Mother.

Mother: Well, darling, are you up, dressed, and ready to begin your day?

Daughter: (*looks at her robe*) Yes, Mother.

Mother: Let's start in the kitchen.
Counters washed?
Stove clean?
Food for supper?
What are you having?
What about vegetables?
Tea towels bleached?
Living room vacuumed?
Dusted?
Doilies straightened?

Daughter is eating potato chips and crunching into the phone.

Mother: Darling, what are you eating?

Daughter: Vegetable tray.

Mother: Wonderful! Now let's continue; this is so exciting!
Bathroom toilet cleaned?
Blue cleaner added to the water?
Bathtub washed?
And rinsed?
Counters cleaned?
Toilet paper on the roll, not just on the back?

Daughter: Mom, now that you've phoned, I could really use some advice on something...

Mother: (*interrupting*) Interrupting – very rude, but very well, go ahead!

Daughter: You remember my boyfriend, Peter?

Mother: (*growls*) Darling, darling, darling, you know what I said when I first met your young man, I don't like him, dump him. So darling, do it. Now, on to my news...

Daughter: But, mom…

Mother: Darling, interrupting again. Now, my news is that after having sacrificed some of my best years in order to support your independent living process, I feel it is time for me to stretch my own wings, and to that end, I am going on a yearlong cruise. Wonderful, wonderful isn't it!

Daughter: But, Mom, who will help me with the things I need?

Mothers: Well, support partners, darling. And you are so independent. Look at this list. It's a five-star report. You'll do fine, darling, you can email me.

Daughter: I don't have a computer.

Mother: Oh, well, then you can't. But a year goes by quickly. Anyway, more about me, me, me. Let me read you my itinerary. Blah, blah…

Daughter rolls her eyes, sticks her tongue out at the phone and walks away.

Mother: Darling, are you listening to me, hello…hello!!! Oh, what an ungrateful girl she is.

Blackout.

Music cue

End of vignette

CHORUS

We like to travel daily.
We like to ride the bus.

We'll cause a little havoc,
And you'll raise a little fuss.
We'll cause some further upset,
And then you'll really cuss.
The chaos will be wild,
But the onus ain't on us.

Vignette 8

Several people are seated on a bus. The driver is reclining and not driving. Two of the people are a couple. The girlfriend is intolerant and always complaining and criticizing, particularly of her boyfriend. The boyfriend can be played meek and frightened of her.

Girlfriend: Honey, why did you wear that shirt? You know I hate it. When we get home, I want you to take it off. For goodness sake, this is the slowest bus I've ever taken. Hey buddy, get a move on.

Driver steps on gas and squeals off with everyone on the bus lurching about. Squeals to a stop.

Passenger 1 enters with a mimed service Dog.

Passenger 2:   Oh look, a working service Dog.

Girlfriend: Dog! A dog on the bus! How unhygienic. They shouldn't be allowed. They should be on their own special buses. I feel an allergic reaction coming on.

Boyfriend: You're not allergic to dogs.

Girlfriend: Shut up.

Passenger 1:   Mind your own business.

Girlfriend: How rude!

Boyfriend tries to pet the dog.

Girlfriend: (*slapping his hand*) Don't touch that animal.

Throughout the rest of the vignette, the boyfriend tries to surreptitiously pet the dog without getting caught.

Girlfriend: La de dah. Still waiting for the BUS TO GO!!!

Squealing of tires and vroom of engine. Screech of brakes. A woman who is blind and her companion are standing at the bus stop.

Blind person: Oh, no! Tell me it's not that crazy French Canadian driver again today?

Assistant: Yeah, it's him.

Blind person: Can we take the next bus?

Assistant: We'll be late. Hey, but here's an idea. You go ahead and find a seat, and I'll slow him down with all my smallest change.

Blind Person: Thanks so much, 'cause if he takes off before I'm seated, my ass will be on the floor.

Person who is blind makes her way down the aisle. As she feels for an empty chair, she inadvertently squeezes a woman's breasts.

Indignant woman: Hey, watch it, lady. I don't swing that way.

Blind person: Sorry, so sorry.

She continues down the aisle and touches the girlfriend's breasts.

Girlfriend: Hey, grow your own!

Blind person: Sorry, sorry, just trying to find a seat.

She waves her hand over the boyfriend and sensing that the seat is empty, proceeds to sit in his lap.

Girlfriend: Hey, get off his lap now.

Boyfriend: (*with enthusiasm*) It's OK. I don't mind.

Girlfriend: I mind!

Blind person: Sorry, sorry.

She finds what appears to be an empty seat and then sits down on a grocery bag, filled with egg cartons, with a tremendous crackling crunch.

Blind person: Oh, no.

Girlfriend: Oh, yes.

Blind person: Your boobs, your boyfriend.

Girlfriend: And my eggs.

Blind person: I am so very, very sorry.

Girlfriend: I am a compassionate person. A very compassionate person. I can see you are blind. (*waves her hand in front of blind woman's eyes*) I can see you can't take care of yourself. BUT! Don't you have someone who gets paid the big bucks to ensure you don't get into trouble?

Assistant: That would be me.

Girlfriend: Yeah, you. Where the hell have you been? Couldn't you have done some more?

Assistant: More? I can always do more.

Assistant picks up the grocery bag, drops it to the floor, and jumps with full force up and down on the contents. He then gingerly picks it up and hands it to the girlfriend.

Assistant: Careful there, it's a bit drippy.

Blind person: I just love it when you do more.

Assistant: Anytime.

Girlfriend: (*looking afraid*) These disabled people frighten me. I told you we need a car. Now our afternoon is in chaos. What do you want to do?

Boyfriend: (*putting his arm around blind woman*) I want a new girlfriend.

Blackout.

Music cue

End of vignette

CHORUS

Oooooooh, hidey hidey hidey hidey hidey hidey hey!
Oh sure, we like to vacuum
When money's to be had.
But coming home to regroup
Makes us happy and so glad.
So, don't get quite so bossy,
And we won't get so mad.
Let us make our own choices

Cause empowerment is rad!

Vignette 9

Characters: Person with Disability (PwD) and two support partners. Scenario: Support Partner 1 is a no-nonsense kind of person. Support Partner 2 is a bleeding heart who feels people with disabilities need to be coddled and protected.

Enter PwD and Support 1.

PwD: Oohhhh, I hurt all over. It was such a difficult day.

Support 1: You've got my sympathy. It was a drag that the vacuum broke at work, and you had to sweep the theatre by hand, but it's done and you can take a break for a while.

PwD: I am going to sit and watch TV all day.

Support 1: No way. We've had this conversation earlier. The agency sent us the notice that the inspectors are coming to look your apartment over tomorrow morning at nine a.m. sharp, and if it isn't up to code, which I can tell you it's not, because you have been totally slack in your maintenance, then your days of independent living are through.

PwD: But I like living on my own.

Support 1:   Well, then, that should be the motivation you need to get this place clean today. And, as well, you have a new daytime support that is coming by today, and she is going to oversee that you get this place together.

PwD: I'll do it tomorrow.

Support 1:   You've used up your tomorrows. Today, or it's group home living for you.

Doorbell rings.

Support 2:   Hi, I'm _____ from the agency.

Support 1:   Great. I'm _____. Have you read the notice?

Support 2:   Inspectors at nine a.m.

Support 1:   Good, well, I'm off to do some errands for a couple of hours and the main responsibility is getting him to clean this place up so it passes inspection.

Support 2:   No problem.

Support 1:   See ya then. (*exits*)

Support 2:   (*surveying the room*) My, my, my, this is a rather untidy place. Hello there. (*in exaggeratedly slow enunciation*) My name is _____ and I am going to be helping you today. Would you like that?

PwD: (*rolls his eyeballs*) I'm supposed to clean this place.

Support: (*in singsong voice*) Well then, let us get started, shall we? Let's start here with all these mouldy clothes. Heave ho and into the laundry basket. Now if you do that every time, they won't form an enormous pile. And what about all these trophies?

PwD: Those are special to me.

Support 2:   This is not your name.

PwD: I buy them second hand. They make me feel special.

Support 2:   How sad. Where do you keep the vacuum?

PwD: In the closet.

Support 2 exits to get vacuum.

PwD: (*rubs his hands gleefully and says to the audience*) I am sure I can take advantage of this situation. (*laughs evilly*)

Support 2:   (*lugs out vacuum*) Well now, here you go.

PwD: I am so stupid. I don't know how to use a vacuum.

Support 2:   No, no, no, you're not stupid. You just haven't been properly trained in life skills. I can help you with that. Now you just take the hose and hit this button

Sound cue: vacuum. Support 2 starts to vacuum the rug. Turns off the vacuum.

Support 2:   Now you give it a try, sweetie.

PwD: I am so sorry. I wasn't paying attention, could you PLEASE show me again?

Support 2:   Well, I suppose I could do the vacuuming today, and you can observe and learn.

PwD: That would be good.

Vacuum cue.

PwD: Coffee? Coffee! COFFEE! (*bellowing*)

Vacuum cue ends.

PwD: Could you please get me a cup of coffee?

Support 2:   Oh, sure I guess.

Returns with coffee and continues to vacuum.

PwD: Sugar! Sugar!

Support 2:   Pardon me?

PwD: I need some sugar.

Support 2:   Oh, of course.

PwD: You are a much nicer person than my morning support.

Support 2:   (*very pleased*) Oh, really?

PwD: And you are much prettier.

Support 2:   Oh, we all can't be blessed. (*fluffs her hair*)

Brings in the sugar.

Vacuum cue.

PwD: (*yelling*) Cookies!

Support 2:   (*trying to conceal her irritation*) What?

PwD: I'm so very hungry, and I haven't had lunch. Could I have a cookie, please?

Support 2:   (*instantly apologetic.*) You haven't had lunch. That's terrible. Of course I'll get you a cookie. Although, this is daytime support's responsibility.

PwD: Three please.

Support 2:   Three.

Returns with the plate of cookies.

Support 2:   Now, I just vacuumed so please try not to spill.

PwD immediately drops cookies.

Support 2:   No matter, let's just sweep this under the carpet.

Support 2:   Now, vacuuming is finished. Do you think in the future you will be able to do this?

PwD: I think so.

Support 2:   Good, we are making lots of progress, I think. Now, let's just finish this up with some spick and span dusting. Where do you keep the rags?

PwD: In the closet.

Support 2: (*brings back rag and spray wax and hands it to PwD*) There you go, let's get at it, sunshine.

PwD: I don't understand how to do this?

Support 2: Have you no life skills? What is daytime support doing?

PwD: I'm so very sorry.

Support 2: This is not your fault. You just don't worry your head about that. That is what I am here to help you with.

PwD: Thank you so much. You smell beautiful.

Support 2: Really. My new French cologne.

Support 2: OK. Now watch me. You just spray … and then rub. Spray … and then rub. It's easy. You have a go.

PwD: My attention wanders so much. Could you show me again?

Support 2: (*sighs*) OK. Spray … rub. Spray … rub.

PwD: I think if I could watch just one more time? Please? Then I would feel really confident.

Support 2: That's what we are aiming for. OK. Spray – rub. Spray – rub. And that about finishes it up. But we are ready for next time. And I'm ready for a break.

Doorbell.

Support 1:   I'm back.

Support 2:   (*with irritation*) We have some things to discuss. (*stomps off*)

Support 1:   What's with her?

PwD: I don't know. She is really crabby. You are much nicer.

Support 1:   True, but then ... oh my Heavens. I don't care how crabby she is. Look at this place. That woman really motivated you.

PwD: I had to do it all by myself.

Support 1:   All by yourself. She was supposed to offer some limited assistance. I'll be speaking with her.

PwD: I don't think I want her to come back.

Support 1:   We can get you a new worker if she is going to be such a slacker. Oh, by the way, you never got to the kitchen, and things are growing wild in there.

PwD: But I'm so tired now.

Support 1:   Listen, you did such an excellent job on the living room, that this time, and this one time only, I'll clean the kitchen for you.

Exits the room.

PwD: (*Big triumph signal with hands and yells*) Yes! (*Blackout*)

Music cue

End of vignette

CHORUS

If CPR's your calling,
We won't give you no lip.
But when you hear us calling,
We ask that you don't slip.
We know that there's confusion
With that old lip to lip.
But there ain't no confusion
When the action's hip to hip.

Vignette 10

One Diane is sitting by herself. Nicky is in a bedroom with a man, under the covers.

Nicky : (*to her boyfriend*) Oh Phillipe, my sweet, how romantic that you snuck into my home. Now that you are here, what do you think we should do?

Boyfriend: You know what I want, baby. Let's do it. (*They throw a bed sheet over their heads.*)

Sound cue in: sexy music. *Sound cue out.*

Diane: (*throws down her magazine.*) My roommate gets all the guys. And what do I get? A stupid magazine.

Sound cue in: sexy music. *Sound cue out.*

Diane: (*with a mischievous look*) But maybe she's in trouble. Maybe I should be getting some help for her. (*picks up phone and dials*)

Support: Hello _____ here.

Diane: Oh hello, this is Diane.

Support: Hi, Diane. How is it going?

Diane: Not too good. I think there is some trouble.

Support: Trouble? What kind of trouble?

Diane: I think Nicky is having sex.

Support: Laughing! Oh, that's a good one. You know the rules. No sex in my group home. But listen, you seem a bit agitated, why don't I drop by and check in on you girls? I'm with Dustin now, but I'll just bring him along. See ya in a minute.

Diane : Thanks. (*hangs up smiling*)

Support: (*entering*) Well, hi, Diane. Dustin, why don't you sit down with Diane? Now Diane, what seems to be the…

Laughter and noise heard from next door.

Support: My, my, that doesn't sound at all right. I'd better investigate.

Opens door to bedroom. Boyfriend hides under the sheets.

Support: Nicky, what are you doing in bed half clad in the middle of the afternoon?

Nicky : I'm hot. It's so hot in here.

Support: It's not hot. In fact, it's cool. And what are you doing? Get your clothes on. Anyone could walk in.

Nicky: They couldn't if I got any privacy.

Support: Privacy ha! Not in my group home. What are you doing in bed in the middle of the afternoon?

Nicky : We are...

Support: What? We?

Nicky : I mean oui. Like in French. Oui oui. Yes. Yes I am ...

Support: Oh, learning French. That's good. A project.

Nicky: Oui.

Support: You know it was pretty loud in here. You have the TV on really loud and what channel are you watching?

Man in bed: Soixante-neuf.

Support: What? Who was that?

Nicky : (*coughing, lowers voice*) Soixante-neuf. You know French. Channel 69.

Support: Oh yeah, French again. Well, listen, you have a cough because you are sitting in bed with your night shirt. You have obviously got a cold.

Nicky : You are right again.

Support: Now I want you to put on some clothes and go out and sit with your roommate for a while. She really likes you, and you could make some more effort.

Nicky : (*coughing*) You are right, but listen, (*cough cough*) with this cold maybe I shouldn't hang with her today. I wouldn't want to give it to her.

Support: OK, then stay in bed and get some rest. Now before I leave I just have a question to ask you. What is it with all these condoms on the floor?

Nicky : Oh, oh, those condoms. Well I am learning French so I can audition to be in Cirque de Soleil, and I am practicing making balloon animals with the condoms.

Support: Isn't that rather expensive?

Nicky: Oh no, they are perfect and cheap.

Support: OK, well, get some rest.

Nicky: We will. I mean oui, oui, I will.

Support leaves.

Nicky : We don't have much time, let's get to it!

Support: (*to roommate*) Well, your roommate is a bit eccentric, but I don't see any real problems. Hey, I've got a couple of errands to run, why don't I leave Dustin here with you for company and I'll come back in an hour for my shift with you both. You might check out channel 69, your roomie was really enjoying it.

Diane and Dustin: Fine.

Support exits.

Diane: Let's do it.

Dustin: Yeah!!!

(*They throw bed sheet over themselves.*)

Sound cue: sexy music.

End of vignette

CHORUS

We like to spend our money.
We like to gamble some.
We even go to Vegas.
We've got savvy, we're not dumb,
But when the chinkin's over,
And we just want to rest

Don't think we want a handout,
Or you we will arrest.

Vignette 11

Straight line of cast members standing with one arm bent as if they are slot machines. Enter woman who is blind, with cup full of change, talking to her offstage companion.

Blind woman: OK, listen I've got a few bucks left here to play the slots with, and then I'll meet you at the bar!

Humming and walking up to machine #1.

The woman moves from machine to machine putting in coins

and pulling levers. Each person gets to endow their machine with a character that in the end pays out nothing to the woman. She reaches the end of the line and is feeling good about her day.

Blind woman: Well, I didn't win a thing, but that's OK, 'cause it's Las Vegas, and the fun doesn't stop.

Enter person who sees blind woman. He is aghast with pity. Walks past and drops change into her cup and says, "Take care with that."

Blind woman: Take care with that? Take care with what? (*shakes her cup and hears the jingle*) Oh, Good Grief! She thought I was begging. I wasn't begging. I have never begged in my life. I am so ... I don't know embarrassed ... But, hey, honest mistake. It's the thought that counts, I guess. What a story for the girls. What a once-in-a-life-time story.

Enter another person who drops change in her cup and says, "You poor, poor dear."

Blind woman: Poor dear? Poor, poor dear? I'll "poor, poor, dear" you one! I am not begging. I can't believe this. What century am I living in? (*starts to yell to the room in general*) I do not need a handout because I am blind. I have a degree. I have two degrees, I am a single mother, and I own my own home. I am the Artistic Director of my own theatre company, I have a boyfriend, and you know what that means, I have sex, lots of it. And I ... I ... Shakes the cup in a curious way. I wonder if I have enough for a drink? (*exits*)

Music cues

End of vignette

CHORUS

You think your life is crazy,
You think you've got it tough,
Well, your future may seem hazy,
And we know you've got it rough.
We know we make you crazy
With all our special stuff,
But, hey there all you Boy Scouts,
Enough is enough.

Vignette 12

The PwD from the initial vignette is sitting in his chair (still) watching TV. The cast members slowly move in on him, chanting phrases from the other vignettes and some like "What are you doing?" "Hurry up!" "You were supposed to be ready!" The words build in intensity until one person shouts his name. Silence.

Support: Hey buddy, whatcha watching?

PwD: "Whose Life is it Anyway?"

Support: (*looking sheepish, mumbling*) He's right, whose life is it?

Group (*on cue*):
Hidey hidey hidey hidey hidey hidey hey
You like to keep us busy
To keep us on the run.
Bowling, swimming, working too and having lots of fun.
But sometimes we're just lazy,
And TV is our friend.
So, let us gaze into the haze,
We'll love ya till the end

THE END

CHAPTER NINE

Maestropiece Theatre

The Political Arena—It's No Joke

The evolution of InsideOut Theatre has been a journey of demystifying the theatre arts. Throughout its history, the company's consistent message, in theory and in practice, has been the right to perform uniquely on theatrical stages of choice. To achieve this goal, InsideOut has collaborated with many mainstream theatre artists. These partnerships have been rich in knowledge and experience and when healthy reciprocity exists, a vibrant and productive collaboration flourishes.

In 2004, InsideOut Theatre effectively collaborated with The Curiously Canadian Improv Guild. As there are differing perceptions of relative status between mainstream theatre and InsideOut, some of these perceptions require examination with respect to collaboration. Some theatre artists perceive themselves as professional, whereas, others fit better within a community theatre model. Many fall somewhere in the middle, and over the years there has been an on-going debate regarding the true nature of each. InsideOut fits easily into either camp but at times this has been uncomfortable because members of each group are threatened by our flexible nature. Typically, community theatre thrives by using volunteer actors and technical support, while professional artists are paid. Membership in organizations like Actors' Equity and ACTRA are often mandatory for the professional. The likelihood of a fruitful relationship can be reached when collaborating theatre companies are equally enthused about the process. An equitable sense of contributing to, as well as learning from, the theatrical collaboration is ideal.

The partnership between InsideOut Theatre and The Curiously Canadian Improv Guild was well balanced on a number of fronts. There was never any question about fee for service (InsideOut facilitators always got paid), but the emphasis was clearly on developing an interesting performance. Actors' Equity was never discussed, and the professional versus amateur debate was not an issue. A discussion founded on such hierarchical assumptions would have been considered counterproductive and irrelevant. Rather, both parties brought their strengths and openness to the stage. InsideOut Theatre provided the material for the performance; the improvisational tweaking stemmed from The Curiously Canadian Improv Guild. Artistic Director of the guild, Rick Hilton, was more than willing to learn about actors with disabilities, and came to the platform with eager enthusiasm. I, as a blind Artistic Director, while providing an already humorously informed script, was more than happy to receive the visual input from the sharp eye of a trained improvisational specialist. That script, *Maestropiece Theatre*, became an audience favourite, often referred to by Rick's witty and politically astute subtitle: *The Severely Normal Theatre Show*. All politics aside, the process was energising and the outcome truly magic.

The maturity of both companies also boded well for a successful collaboration. Even though The Curiously Canadian Improv Guild was itself embryonic, Rick Hilton possessed thirty years of seasoned improvisational training and performing. InsideOut Theatre, as a company, had evolved through years of performing locally and abroad. The need to struggle for control tends to diminish when confidence and maturity are evident.

A final point regarding the successful collaboration between InsideOut Theatre and The Curiously Canadian Improv Guild resides in the inherent human need for laughter. The seasoned improv specialist is trained in the art of funny business and, as much as 'art is life'; improv is life, but bigger and funnier. Nevertheless, laughter is actually very serious business.[37] InsideOut performances have always conveyed serious messages through humour. And, our productions have always been improv-inspired, so the leap to a successful collaboration with an improv specialist was short. In a meaningful phrase: "a small step for InsideOut Theatre; a large leap for the theatre community."

Humour, Trickster, and Social Change Artists

Reference has been made to the humorous delivery of a serious message throughout this book, but its importance deserves special attention. Loretta LaRoche, a leading stress management expert, asks, "Guess what we can't have too much of? That's right, laughter."[38] This quotation is a poignant expression of the InsideOut trademark, namely humour. Humour is our weapon of choice, but this is also true throughout the Disability Theatre movement. Taylor says that there are similarities both psychological and physical "between the effect of humour – laughter, and one effect of the sacred – ecstasy. Both have the feeling that they come from behind the subject and indicate that a force outside the ego is in control."[39] We are all familiar with forces outside our ego being in control; it is part of that dynamic state that is not here, not there, but in-between, where performers and audiences meet.

Influenced by Feminism, InsideOut has always used a cooperative practice and has continuously experienced defining moments through the power of humour; challenging convention both within mainstream theatre arts and with the

---

[37] As Taylor observes, "There are a number of physical and psychological similarities, too, between the effect of humour – laughter, and one effect of the sacred – ecstasy" (p. 79).

[38] LaRoche, Loretta. *Life Is Short – Wear Your Party Pants: Ten Simple Truths That Lead to an Amazing Life.* Audio CD.

[39] Taylor, p. 79.

public. Zen Buddhist teachers know that "What is funny can be used as a tool for opening the mind of the apprentice monk."[40] The Shamanic tradition also recognises that the fool, or the clown, "embodies, at one and the same time, the most direct and the most disguised representation of the heart source of the show: the shaman himself (herself)."[41] When considering these various thematic threads, the archetype of Trickster repeatedly comes to mind.

Trickster energy[42] is the very stuff that pushes society to the fringes and beyond. Without it, we remain complacent, comfortable, and conventional. Laura Kerr describes the trickster energy succinctly: "Trickster saved me from my old antic of trying to impose order on the world, reminding me to question assumptions and practices…The Trickster has been depicted as both mythical figure and archetype, or what C. G. Jung identified as instinctual patterns for behaviour. As archetype, Trickster is a masterful, yet unpredictable catalyst of psychological change. Trickster energy challenges staid belief systems and well-worn habits by unearthing unconscious assumptions and toppling worldviews that have lost their usefulness. However, there is nothing moralistic about the Trickster. Sometimes in order to continually grow, things simply have to change."[43]

The important work of Trickster coupled with underworld initiation frees us as a society from stagnation and, ultimately, elimination. Historically many civilizations have risen and then fallen because of an inability to adapt to changes in the environment. Perhaps had they embraced the Trickster energy, they would still be thriving today.

---

[40] Taylor, p. 79.
[41] Taylor, p. 80.
[42] As described by Carl Jung, Caroline W. Casey, Ricki Stefanie Tannen, et al.
[43] The Trickster Will Have its Way
http://www.laurakkerr.com/2011/02/06/the-trickster-will-have-its-way/February 2012

Ricki Stephanie Tannen, in her book *The Female Trickster*, states that women's humour, and the humour of other minorities, tends to be subversive: a means of challenging the powerful. She believes for this reason, the female Trickster "is more dangerous than the traditional Trickster" who challenges boundaries but leaves them intact. "Where the traditional Trickster lets off steam by playing at the margins, the female Trickster...deconstructs the margins and enters new terrain."[44] Tannen addresses one of the issues pervasive within minorities, including people with disabilities, but not always acknowledged: anger.

When confronted with an angry person, most of us try to smooth things over and withdraw from the situation, or we get angry in turn and escalate anger into conflict. Communication is difficult to achieve when people are overtly angry. Tannen suggests that humour "can clear a space within an unhappy situation... As an alternative to complaining about a situation, using humour can make it easier for the dominant culture to integrate dissention."[45] Anger must be expressed, or it can turn into depression or other physical disorders but the Trickster expresses anger creatively with humour, which allows the angry person to vent and provides the listener with the opportunity to change.

The work of Caroline W. Casey, social activist, astrologer, and visionary, has been valuable in understanding the relationship between the InsideOut process and the importance of the Trickster archetype. "Trickster god energy" as Casey refers, is essential for ensuring a thriving community. She identifies those who possess this energy as "social change artists." Superficially, social change artists might be perceived as "mavericks or rebels"[46] but a deeper investigation reveals a truth more fundamental to the evolution of humanity than one would first suspect.

---

[44] Tannen, Ricki Stefanie. *The Female Trickster*. p. 159.

[45] Tannen, p. 167.

[46] Casey, Caroline. *Making the Gods Work for You.*

Consider the first members of the human tribe who insisted that fire might be a useful tool if it could be tamed, that employing the wheel was superior to dragging heavy objects that boiling the jars before canning the fruit prevented sickness, that women and men are equally valuable, or that all human beings are born "equal in dignity."[47] These advances within the human community would not have been made without social change artists.

Casey further describes all theatre as intrinsically transformative.[48] She goes on to say we know we're supposed to get something from theatre, so when we don't, the urge is to get bigger and louder rather than simply staying with the process until transformation has occurred. Conventionally, theatre is often one step from transformation, a step that indeed has been taken by the InsideOut practice. The proof of this lies in 'active rather than passive' participation. While conventional thinkers view actors with disabilities on stage as challenging, the faithful followers of the InsideOut experience realise the movement as a necessary liberation.

According to Casey, people without imaginative passion fall under the influence of what she calls the "toxic mimic", which is an external pressure that demands unquestioning conformity. Gangs or cults are examples of such external pressures. When people join these types of organizations, they are prevented from thinking for themselves and finding their own creative solutions. They rigidly follow the organizations' rules, often to their own destruction. Casey points out the need for us to be active in finding our passion, rather than passively merging with a stifling organization. At InsideOut we strive to spark disabled actors to find their own creative passion. This is in contrast to hours of television viewing, watching others perform or worse yet,

---

[47] Universal Declaration of Human Rights. http://www.un.org/Overview/rights.html. March 2007.
[48] Casey, Caroline. *Making the Gods Work for You.*

joining unscrupulous organizations where they would be victimized. We invite the Trickster, who incites us to go against the status quo, who instead shows us to follow our passion to explore new territory.

Traditionally, every culture has in one way or another honoured the important, albeit often challenging influence of what is referred to as Trickster. The Trickster phenomenon is recognised in a variety of symbols including rabbit, raven, the planet Uranus, and others. The symbol of coyote is a favourite. Coyote can be seen skulking in the shadowy background of all InsideOut performances by those audience members who have a trained eye in the Shamanic world. For the audience members who are not educated in the ways of Trickster, they, too, will be subconsciously aware and feeling its edgy presence. Coyote can be found lurking in the background on the cover of this book, but then again, what is seen might be the service dog, which made its debut in the three-city Fringe Festival tour. Or it may be a wolf. Perhaps there's nothing there at all; you decide. The imagination is a wonderful and powerful tool for accessing the multiple layers of the truth. In that spirit of symbol and imagination, Shamanism is represented by the image of a turtle. Again, the turtle is only one symbol of many that represents Shamanism. Turtle, also appears on the cover of this book.

Disability Theatre challenges conventional thinking and pushes the borders of complacency and stagnation. InsideOut Theatre is destined to be an agent of social change: building community, nurturing the Trickster spirit, and encouraging 'active' participation. And we're darn funny to boot! Enjoy the Finale!

MAESTROPIECE THEATRE

Ruth and Rick stand centre stage (CS), side-by-side, arms linked.

Ruth: (*to Rick*) You have a story.

Rick: Yes, I do. In fact, it comes from my parking cars outside here, and I'm going to ask Ruth to do an improv with me, which she's only done once before in her life. So we're going to do a little improvisation, on the spot.

Ruth, stand behind me and put your arms through my arms. (*Ruth moves behind Rick and puts her arms under his, while he links his hands behind him.*) I'm going to be the speaker, and you're going to be my arms, all right? I'd like to tell you the story of how I arrived here at this theatre.

During the story, Ruth gestures with her arms as though she were telling the story, using broad movements to express emotion and mime action in response to what Rick says. The audience provides crowd noises.

So, I woke up one morning, sprang out of bed, ran to the car and I put in the key and I drove like a maniac! (*Ruth covers his eyes.*) I drove like I was blind. People were yelling at me. I got angry because I wasn't able to find the theatre; I got very flustered. I didn't care. I was going to the InsideOut show, and I didn't care if it was in an alley, I was going to drive like a maniac. But the rest of the city got really, really mad at me. So I hung a BIG left turn (*screech*) and got on a gravel road and there was me, waving people in! Thank you very much!

Ruth: So we have had – in case you haven't noticed – a tremendous amount of fun putting this show together. We hope you have fun, too. We love your applause, we love your laughter – you're going to have to laugh loud in order to laugh louder than Rick and I do, even though we've seen the show many times – and we love you. So thank you very much for coming and enjoy!

Rick and Ruth exit.

Impossible? Not for a Modern Woman

Suspenseful theme music plays throughout the entire vignette; lights come up on a single stool CS. Two actors enter, one has his hands tied behind his back and is being forced to sit on the stool while the other mimes tying him to it.

Actor 1: Help! Help!

Actor 2: *Laughs evilly, gags Actor 1, places a box labelled BOMB on his lap, exits.*

Suspenseful theme starts again. Actor 3 enters, dressed like a Trade Show Model or magician's assistant. She holds up cards with numbers starting at 10 and counts down the seconds until the bomb will explode. At card 9, the Heroine enters, wearing a red cape. As the count down continues, Actor 1 struggles, and the Heroine approaches him.

Heroine: *Sees the bomb, comforts Actor 1, takes the bomb and puts it DSL (downstage left), unties Actor 1 and, as the countdown reaches 2 and 1, the actors all exit; Actor 1 carries the stool. Bomb explodes on empty stage. End of vignette*

Speak Now or Forever Hold Your Peace

Sound of birds chirping as lights come up on park bench. Two women enter SL.

Female Aide: Is this the right park bench, Diane?

Diane: Yes.

Female Aide: Would you like for me to stay with you?

Diane: (*pointing USL*) Go!

Female Aide runs offstage. Diane sits on the bench. Two men enter SR.

Male Aide: Is there anything else I can do for you?

Andrew: No.

Male Aide: Would you like to sit on that park bench?

Andrew: (*eagerly as he sees Diane*) Yes. (*Diane pats the bench invitingly.*)

Male Aide: Are you sure?

Andrew: (*nodding and moving towards the bench*)

Male Aide: Because I can find another one.

Andrew: (*firmly, turns his back*) This is ok.

Male Aide: Are you sure there isn't anything else I can do for you? Nothing at all?

Andrew: (*waving him away*) Nothing.

Male Aide: You'll call me if there is anything?

Andrew: (*impatient*) Yes, yes.

Male Aide: All right. (*turns to leave, then turns back*) I'll just be right over here.

(*exits SR*)

Andrew: Fine, ok! (*sits on the bench*)

Diane moves closer to him, and they begin to snuggle. She plays with Andrew's hair.

Andrew: Wow! Hmmm! (*shyly looking at Diane*) You look pretty.

Diane: (*excited*) Do I look pretty? Thanks! Yes, I do look pretty, I know.

(*continues to stroke his hair, he makes appreciative noises*)

Andrew: (*reaching into his pocket*) I… I have something to ask you.

Diane: Oh? Go ahead.

Andrew: (*takes out a ring box and goes down on one knee*) Will…

Diane: Will?

Andrew: You…

Diane: You?

Andrew: Marry me?

Diane: (*thrilled*) Will I marry you? I… I…

Nicky enters from SR and Lindsay enters from SL. They are wearing white lab coats.

Nicky: Wrong, wrong, wrong. This so wrong.

Lindsay: It *is* wrong. (*patting Diane's head*) Poor Diane! She's being taken advantage of, and she doesn't understand.

Diane pulls away from Lindsay, who keeps trying to pat her shoulder.

Nicky: No, that's not what I mean! There are two people with disabilities on the same bench in the same park! This is wrong. They need… Hold on! (*reaches into her pocket and takes out a calculator and starts punching numbers*) For our quota and true integration, they need twenty people without disabilities!

Lindsay: You know what they need? They need to be in a safe environment with two people with disabilities – with their support partners – that's what they need. *(looks around for the aides)*

Nicky: (*looking around*) Where are their support partners?

Lindsay: (*patting Andrew's shoulder, pulls on Diane's arm*) There, there. We'll make sure no one takes advantage of either of you. (*to Nicky*) They require supervision…

Nicky: (*takes a notebook from her pocket*) No, no, I have this written down in my little book. (*reads and shows book to Lindsay*) True integration is when one person with a disability is joined by nine people without disabilities. (*shuts book and returns it to her pocket*) So, I'm going to take Andrew, and we're going to look for nine non-disabled people.

Lindsay: No, no, they do not need that. They need to be in a safe environment together so they can have their relationship…

Nicky: (*scandalized*) Relationship! Are you crazy?

Lindsay: What's wrong? They're people, too, and…. Oh! Wait! Baby!

Nicky: Yeah, they could have a baby. (*she and Lindsay talk to each other over Diane's and Andrews' heads*)

Lindsay: A baby!

Nicky: What if it's a baby with disabilities? (*Lindsay gasps*) Hold on! (*takes out calculator*) Then we'd need *thirty* people without disabilities! (*He grabs Andrew and tries to pull him away; Lindsay is pulling Diane in the opposite direction.*) We need to get them away…

Diane: Shut up!

Nicky and Lindsay stop pulling and jump back.

Nicky/Lindsay: Whoa!

Lindsay: Isn't she uppity?

Nicky: (*crosses behind bench to join Lindsay*) Attitude, attitude.

Lindsay: Well! We'll just go where we're appreciated.

Nicky: Don't come complaining to us if this doesn't work out.

Lindsay: And it never does! (*They exit SL.*)

Diane: Yes, Andrew, I will marry you.

Andrew: Yahoo!

Dianne: (*to audience*) How many of you are coming to my wedding? You're all invited, but you have to be on time! Just let me know, and don't forget the presents.

Andrew and Diane exit hand-in-hand.

Take Five

Relaxing theme music plays throughout this vignette. Lights come up on Carmen (SR) facing Andrew (SL), each standing behind a stool. On the woman's stool is a feather boa, and on the man's stool there is a black jacket. Both actors are in a neutral stance. Diane enters SR and Greg enters SL; he is wearing a dressing gown. Diane stands in front of Carmen, Greg in front of Andrew. This is a mirror exercise. Diane and Greg prepare for a date, for example, Greg brushes his teeth, shaves, etc., and Andrew mirrors Greg's actions. Diane puts on make-up, examines her teeth, does her hair and Carmen mirrors her actions. The actors have fun with this.

Diane mimes zipping up her dress. She picks up one end of the boa lying on the stool and wraps her end around her neck. Carmen picks up the other and wraps her end around her own neck. They have a tug of war and shake their fingers at each other. Diane mimes demanding the entire boa until finally Carmen gives up her end and exits SR. Diane wraps the boa around her.

Meanwhile, Greg ties his tie and takes off the dressing gown, hands it to Andrew, who hangs it over his arm. When Greg puts on the jacket, Andrew continues to mime a mirror reaction. Then Greg waves good-bye to Andrew; Andrew 'reflects' the wave and exits SL.

The stools now become "cars." Greg gets into his car and starts driving with a lot of energy, miming going fast. Diane gets in her car but cannot get it started. After several attempts, Diane gets out of her car. A policeman enters SL making the noise of a siren and motions Greg to stop. While Diane kicks the tires, etc., the policeman mimes reprimanding Greg who indicates that he is late. He has a headache; he didn't realize how fast he was going, etc. The policeman is not impressed.

Diane, meanwhile, has decided to hitch a ride and walks around SR with her thumb out. The policeman writes Greg a ticket and exits. Greg gets out of the car and goes to far SL, turns and faces Diane. From far SR, Diane turns and faces Greg. They walk towards each other in slow motion, arms outstretched but cannot quite meet. All the other actors now enter dancing and separate Diane and Greg, leading Diane towards SR and Greg towards SL, dancing and twirling them away from each other. Diane and Greg struggle to unite but are kept apart by the others until by the end of the music, when they finally meet and dance offstage together.

I understand, but do you?

The light comes up on two stools, one SR and one SL. Carmen is sitting on the stool SR.

Carmen: (*using different emphases*) I understand. I understand. I understand.

Greg enters, picks up SL stool and moves it closer to Carmen.

Greg: Hey, how are you doing? Oh, man, I was….uh…last night; it was terrible.

Carmen: I understand.

Greg: You understand? I've got three problems, Ms. Counsellor – three problems. The first one is my mom and the garbage. I *hate* taking out the garbage because it smells *so bad*!

Carmen: I understand.

Greg: Oh, you understand? How about this one? I went to the doctor's office, and I was feeling so bad – I had a cold. And I went to the doctor's office, and he gave me some medicine…

Carmen: (*soothing*) I understand.

Greg: (*annoyed*) You understand? I threw up all over the place.

Carmen: How did that make you feel?

Greg: (*jumping up*) How did that make me feel?! B A double D – BAD! BAD!

Carmen: I understand.

Greg: (*frustrated*) You understand?! You understand!? I don't… I can't…

Carmen: What about a volunteer?

Greg: I don't *want* a volunteer!

Nicky enters from SR. Lindsay enters from SL. Both are wearing white lab coats. Lindsay massages Greg's shoulders while Nicky shakes a finger at him.

Nicky: You ungrateful boy! Volunteers are the foundation of our society.

Greg: Who are you?

Lindsay: (*makes the letter "L" with her fingers and holds to her forehead*) Volunteers are losers!

Nicky: (*aghast*) What?

Lindsay: They're losers – busybodies! Poking their noses in other people's business.

Nicky: No, no, no. They are saints…

Lindsay: (*interrupting*) Without a life! Saints without a life.

Nicky: They are donating their time! And their energy!

Lindsay plays an imaginary violin and mimes wiping tears from her eyes.

Nicky: We couldn't live without them!

Lindsay: We could sure try!

Nicky: No! They are saints.

Lindsay: Aha! I bet you're a volunteer yourself, aren't you? Loser!

Nicky: I'm a saint as well. Volunteers are saints!

Lindsay: Losers!

Nicky and Lindsay now face each other, forgetting Greg and Carmen.

Nicky: Saints!

Lindsay: Losers!

Nicky: Saints!

Lindsay: Losers!

Their voices change into squawks, and they begin to act like chickens, moving to the back of the stage and exit.

Greg: (*holding his head*) Ow! Ow!

Carmen: (*patting his hand*) There, there, it's only the chickens – again!

Greg: Where were we before they came in?

Carmen: I'll get you a volunteer next week. (*stands and exits SR*)

Greg: Yeah – she better be pretty! (*exits SL still holding his head*)

Music plays: Upbeat rock music

Innocent Until Proven Guilty

As the lights come up, relaxing theme music is playing; there is one stool SL and one stool SR. Two separate scenes are played using each stool. Diane, wearing an apron and carrying a rolling pin, enters SL; she slaps the rolling pin against her hand. Robert, wearing a detectives hat and carrying a large magnifying glass, enters SL; he is yawning. The action, all mimed, proceeds in synch with the music. Theme music shifts to suit the mounting tension throughout.

Robert sits on his stool and mimes taking a drink, glancing at his watch, and reading a newspaper. Diane also sits; she mimes waiting impatiently with many glances at her watch.

Greg enters SR obviously sneaking into the house. He is taken aback to find Diane waiting for him. He tries to appease her. She lets him know she can smell the liquor on his breath. She points to her watch. He explains. She does not believe him and is angry. He falls to her feet, begging forgiveness. She is unmoved and points to lip stick on his collar as the music reaches a crescendo, she begins to mime beating Greg with her rolling pin; he falls to the floor. She ends with a stab of the rolling pin, and Greg lies still. She checks his pulse – first one arm, then the other. She does a little dance of joy.

Again in time to the music, she gets an idea and runs next door to where Robert is sitting asleep in his chair. She knocks on the door. He answers and finds her sobbing. He invites her in, pats her shoulder and offers her a seat on his stool. Diane mimes that a woman (making the shape in the air) has killed Diane's husband and points to SR. She has to repeat this a couple of times until Robert understands. He gestures that he will go with her to check this out. He walks across the stage, Diane follows him, dancing. Then Robert turns suddenly and holds up his magnifying glass, but by the time he has turned, Diane is sobbing into her hands. They do this several times as they cross to her house and enter. He is suspicious but cannot catch her dancing.

Robert is horrified when he sees Greg lying on the floor. As he examines the body with his magnifying glass, Diane again dances behind his back, but whenever he turns, she has her hands over her face as though she is crying. Robert is more suspicious but cannot catch her dancing. He examines the rolling pin and finally stands up. Then he points to the body, the rolling pin, and her. She is surprised – what, you accuse me? Then she turns and runs with him following, waving for her to stop. They run across the stage and around the stool SL. Finally he catches her, sits her on the stool, and puts on hand cuffs. They exit SL.

Carmen enters SR; she is wearing a red feather boa. She touches Greg on the shoulder. He sits up, and she helps him to stand. They embrace and exit SL smiling. Lights down as the music ends.

The Passion of the Theatre Arts

The lights come up on five stools arranged CS. Four actors enter, yawning and stretching. Then the Teacher enters SR. The bell rings to start class

Teacher: (*speaking in a nasal, monotone*) Good afternoon, class. I am Professor Hardin, and this afternoon we are going to study about the Passion of Theatre.

All students groan and let their heads fall back as though they have fallen asleep.

Teacher: But first, I would like to introduce a new student.

Greg: (*entering from SL*) Hi, everyone. (*carries a book and is smiling*)

Teacher: Class, this is Greg Ransome. Greg has "Special Needs."

Greg stops smiling, shakes his head, puts the book in front of his face, and waves his hand "No" as the teacher continues.

Teacher: Greg will require a Special Friend to *assist* him.

All the students turn away from the teacher and put their hands up to shield their faces.

Teacher: Are there any volunteers? (*No one responds.*) Well, Greg, perhaps you could choose your own Special Friend. (*waits*)

Greg: (*after a pause, shrugs and points to Diane*) Her.

All the students except Diane give each other a "hi five;" Greg sits on the remaining stool.

Teacher: Thank you. Now as I was saying, this afternoon we're going to study about the passion of theatre.

As the teacher speaks, her voice becomes more monotone, and the students all begin to yawn and nod off again. Nicky enters SR and Lindsay enters SL wearing lab coats as before. During the scene they speak mainly to each other

Nicky/Lindsay: No, no, no.

(*Nicky comes to CS behind the students, and Lindsay comes forward to stand by Greg.*)

Lindsay: This is tokenism at its worst. Poor Number Ten! Number Ten feels *so* uncomfortable. Here (*takes Greg's arm to pull him to his feet*) you come with...

Nicky: (*interfering*) No! Number Ten is staying. It's the class that needs to adapt to Number Ten's needs.

Lindsay: (*to Nicky*) Number Ten would be more comfortable in a secluded environment (*pats Greg's head*). Come with me.

Nicky: *(pushing Greg into his seat)* No, no. Number Ten is fine here. This is good integration.

Lindsay: *(pulling Greg up)* For whom? Come with me.

Nicky: *(pushing Greg into his seat)* Number Ten is fine.

Lindsay: *(pulling Greg up)* No, he's not; come with me.

Nicky: *(pushing Greg into his seat)* Number Ten is staying.

Lindsay: *(pulling Greg up)* No, he's not; come with me.

Nicky: *(pushing Greg into his seat)* Number Ten is staying.

Greg: Wait! Wait! *(stands up and away from both Nicky and Lindsay)* My name is not Number Ten. My name is Greg. Besides I don't need you two. I'm staying right here. Shoo! Shoo! Shoo fly!

Nicky: *(taken aback)* Well!

Lindsay: *(also taken aback)* Of all the... *(turns to Nicky)* Let's go talk to Number Eleven.

Nicky: *(to Greg)* Number Eleven is way nicer than you. *(Lindsay, Nicky exit SL)*

Greg: Good-bye! *(sits down)*

The bell rings, and the other students jump up and run off SR.

Teacher: Class! Class!

Greg: *(opening his book)* Well, as I always say: All's well that ends well!

Music plays: School's Out *by Alice Cooper*

Saloon Soap Opera

Cowboy theme plays as the lights come up on three stools SR. All action is done in relation to the music throughout. Andrew, Steve, and Richard enter SL. Steve and Richard are cowboys coming into the saloon; they each carry a bag of gold dust. Steve and Richard go to the stools. Andrew is the bartender; he goes CS and begins wiping the bar, polishing glasses, etc. Diane and Carmen enter, wearing feather boas; they are the saloon girls. Greg is SR miming riding a horse.

Steve and Richard mime throwing back drinks and demanding more; they vocalize but in gibberish. Diane and Carmen stand behind the men watching. Greg dismounts and enters the saloon. He too starts throwing back drinks. After a couple minutes, he walks over to the other men. They stare at each other and then gesture for him to join them. He sits.

They start playing cards. After a few discards and draws, Steve draws a card from his boot. Greg challenges him. Steve and Richard both get defensive. They posture, and then Greg and Steve with Richard challenge each other to a duel. Greg walks SL as Steve and Richard raise their guns. Greg draws his gun as he turns and shoots them both, and they fall dead.

Diane and Carmen step forward and pick up the bags of gold dust from Steve and Richard. They cross to SL where Greg and Andrew mount their horses and then give each woman a hand up, and as the song ends, they ride across the stage and exit SR.

So You Think You Want To Volunteer?

The lights come up with Ruth sitting in a chair SL. There is a couch CS.

Ruth: (*in the middle of talking with herself*) … and I have to be grateful – that's the worst part. It's not the help so much; it's having to be *grateful*.

While she is talking, Richard appears SR, mimes knocking and entering at a door.

Richard: Hello? (*sits on the couch*)

Ruth: Oh, you startled me. Honestly, make a little noise when you come in so a person knows you're there! So, you're here for an appointment because you want to work with people who are blind. Is that correct?

Richard: Yes.

Ruth: We'll see! I have some hypothetical scenarios that I want you to respond to.

Richard: (*mimes being nervous*)

Ruth: Number one: You are a hairdresser. A blind woman comes to your station. She clearly requests blonde highlights, but *you* think she would look much better as a brunette. What do you do? A. Honour her wishes, or B. Satiate your own artistic temperament.

From behind the couch, an Angel with a halo and a Devil with horns pop up on each side of Richard. These two actors improvise their dialogue, but an example is given here. The Angel and Devil should be as outrageous and funny.

Devil: You make her brunette.

Angel: Your heart should be full of light, and you should listen to her.

Devil: You should choose whatever colour you like.

Angel: No, you honour her wishes.

Devil: Blue, red, green…

Angel: No, she wants blonde.

Devil: She's blind; she won't know.

Angel: Honour her.

Devil: You know what you should do? Shave it!

Angel: No! Your mother wouldn't want you to do that.

Devil: Bald!

Angel: Remember your mother!

Devil: Bald.

Angel: Mother.

The Angel and the Devil struggle, pulling Richard this way and that until he can't stand it any more, and he leans forward with his head in his hand. The Angel and Devil disappear behind the couch. Throughout this struggle, Ruth has sat patiently waiting for an answer.

Richard: (*sitting up*) I feel like a glass of water.

Ruth: Is there something wrong with you? Number two: You have a friend. She's blind. She's the Artistic Director of her own theatre company. You want to impress her. So you tell her that you're going to come see her upcoming production but you don't really want to go – so you don't. What do you do? A. Confess or B. Send her an email the next day telling her just how much you enjoyed the performance.

The Angel and Devil appear from behind the couch.

Devil: You lie!

Angel: You confess! Confession is good for you.

Devil: You had better things to do.

Angel: You can get absolution. And redemption.

Devil: She wouldn't know you weren't in the audience.

Angel: Truth is sacred.

Devil: She's blind. She wouldn't know.

Angel: Your mother would know.

Devil: Lie!

Angel: Confess!

They pull Richard back and forth, miming that they are yelling until finally…

Devil: You lie!

Angel: Truth!

Devil: You lie!

Angel: Truth!

Devil: Lie!

Angel: Truth!

Back and forth until Richard's head is spinning. Then he leans forward, puts his head in his hands, tearing his hair, and they disappear behind the couch. Ruth is waiting.

Richard: (*sitting up*) I'm hungry.

Ruth: Are you *sure* you want to do this? (*Richard is silent.*) Number three: This same friend, who is blind and the Artistic Director of her own theatre company, needs to send out a flyer advertising her upcoming performance. You are helping her. It has been suggested to you that the flyer is unnecessarily negative in its tone. What do you do? A. Leave well enough alone or B. Tactfully suggest that she "lighten up."

Angel and Devil appear once more.

Devil: Screw her!

Angel: No! No!

Devil: Screw her!

Angel: We want people to like us.

Devil: You should put on that flyer whatever you want.

Angel: We want people to come to the show.

Devil: You want a bigger audience? Naked people.

Angel: No! No naked people.

Devil: Boobies.

Angel: Never.

Devil: Sex.

Angel: Chastity.

Devil: Boobies.

Angel: Sweaters.

Devil: Boobies.

Angel: Sweaters.

They pull Richard this way and that between them. The Angel takes off her halo and hits the Devil with it. They abandon Richard, and he leans forward tearing his hair. Shrieking, the Angel and Devil grapple with each other briefly, then disappear behind the couch.

Richard: (*sits up*) Do you want to go for supper?

Ruth: (*sits still for a moment, staring; then slowly puts on her dark glasses, snaps open her cane and stands*) Are you...? (*pause*) I'll get my purse. (*she exits SL*)

Richard: (*stands and makes a "victory" gesture*) Yahoo!

The Angel and Devil also jump up.

Devil: Follow her!

Angel: Be a gentleman.

Devil: She wants you.

Angel: Be respectful.

Richard exits SL with the Devil and Angel arguing on either side of him.

Girl Power

As the lights come up, sad. lonely theme song is playing. There is a chair CS. Behind the chair in a line, the cast members (with the men wearing skirts and wigs) perform synchronized movements to the music. Carmen moves from SR, across stage and back to the chair; she sits and weeps. The "girls" mime misery. Then as the music segues into upbeat Feminist music, Lindsay and Nicky come forward, take Carmen by the arms, pull her up, and start dancing with her and everybody dances with everyone else.

That song fades and soft romantic theme song begins. Greg enters from SL, jumps up on the chair and flexes his muscles and preens. Carmen fawns on him admiringly. The rest of the "girls" mock Greg – flexing their muscles or signalling "loser." Soft romantic music is replaced by upbeat male chauvinistic tune? Greg jumps down from the chair and runs around the stage miming that he is pinching the "girls'" derrieres; they react by jumping and squealing.

Now upbeat Feminist theme song begins to play, and the women shake their fingers at Greg as he backs away from them around the stage and he exits SL. The women continue dancing.

Next is the chorus from upbeat Feminist theme song as the "girls" turn their backs to the audience. The song segues into more upbeat Feminist theme music, and the "girls" synchronize gestures, and then turn and dance.

As this song proceeds, the cast begins to clap in time to the music and, forming a line, they dance off SL.

The End

Works Cited

Bieber, Ruth. "The Truth about Theatre from the InsideOut." *Canadian Theatre Review* 122 (2005) : 55-61.

Brown, Ivan and Roy I. Brown. *Quality of Life and Disability: An Approach for Community Practitioners.* London: Jessica Kingsley, 2003.

Brown, Roy I. and Eddie Bullitis. "The Process of Mental Imagery in Persons With or Without Intellectual Disability: An Exploratory Project." *Journal on Developmental Disabilities*, vol.12, (2006) no. 1, supplement 2:1-18.

Casey, Caroline W. *Making the Gods Work for You: The Astrological Language of the Psyche.* Three Rivers Press, 1999. Audiocassette.

Elkins, James. *The Object Stares Back: On the Nature of Seeing.* New York: Harcourt Brace, 1997.

Gardner, Howard. *Intelligence Reframed: Multiple Intelligences for the 21st Century.* New York: Basic Books, 1999.

Gilligan, Carol. *In a Different Voice: Psychological Theory and Women's Development.* Cambridge, Massachusetts: Harvard University Press, 1982.

Goffman, Erving. *Asylums: Essays on the Social Situation of Mental Patients and Other Inmates.* New York: Doubleday, 1961.

Goffman, Erving. *Stigma: Notes on the Management of Spoiled Identity.* New York: Simon &Schuster, 1963.

Gubar, Susan. "The Blank Page" and the Issues of Female Creativity. *Critical Inquiry,* vol.   8 (1981) :243-63.

Kerr, Laura. *Laura Kerr PhD, IMFT | Trauma's Labyrinth* http://www.laurakkerr.com/about/

LaRoche, Loretta. *Life Is Short – Wear Your Party Pants: Ten Simple Truths That Lead to an Amazing Life.* Carlsbad, California: Hay House, 2003. Audio CD.

Taylor, Rogan, P. *The Death and Resurrection Show: From Shaman to Superstar.* London: Anthony Blond, 1985.

Wolfensberger, Wolf. *A Brief Introduction to Social Role Valorisation: A High-Order   Concept for Addressing the Plight of Societally Devalued People, and for Structuring Human Services.* 3rd ed. Syracuse, New York: Training Institute for Human Service   Planning, Leadership and Change Agency, Syracuse University, 1998.

Reading List

Abbas, Jihan., et al. *Lights...Camera...Attitude: Introducing Disability Arts and Culture*. Toronto: Ryerson RBC Institute for Disability Studies Research and Education.   Ryerson University, 2004.

Amies, Bert, Bernie Warren, and Rob Watling. *Social Drama*. London: John Clare Books,   1986.

Blatner, H. Adam, M.D. *Acting in Practical Applications of Psychodramatic Methods*. New York: Springer Publishing Company, 1973.

Booth, David W. and Charles J. Lundy. *Improvisation: Learning Through Drama*. London: Harcourt Brace Jovanovich, 1985.

Brown, Ivan and Roy I. Brown. *Quality of Life and Disability: An Approach for Community Practitioners*. London:Jessica Kingsley, 2003.

Emunha, Renee. *Acting For Real. Drama Therapy Process, Technique, and Performance*.   New York:Brunner/Mazel Inc., 1994.

Fanelli, Leslie. *Frederick Law Olmsted: Naturalist Landscape Architect* (Written via the lens   of Multiple Intelligences). Unpublished. Utilised in tandem with her touring musical play, *The Promise of Central Park,* 2010.

Fleischer, Doris Zames and Frieda Zames. *The Disability Rights Movement*. Philidelphia: Temple University Press, 2003.

Gardner, Howard. *Five Minds for the Future. Boston, MA:* Harvard Business School Press,   2007.

Gardner, Howard. *Frames of Mind: The Theory of Multiple Intelligences.* New York: Basic   Books, 1983. Basic Books Paperback, 1985. Tenth Anniversary Edition with new introduction, Basic Books, 1993.

Humphries, Tom and Carol Paddon. *Inside Deaf Culture.* Cambridge, MA: Harvard   University Press, 2005.

Johnstone, Keith. *Impro: Improvisation and the Theatre.* London: Eyre Methuen Ltd., 1981.

Levitt, Gina. *No Handicap to Dance. Creative Improvisation for People with Handicaps.*   Cambridge, MA: Brookline Books, 1984.

Spolin, Viola. *Theatre Games for the Classroom.* Illinois: Northwestern University Press, 1986.

Tomlinson, Richard. *Disability, Theatre, and Education.* London: Souvenir Press, 1982.

Warren, Bernie. *Using the Creative Arts in Therapy and Healthcare: A Practical Introduction.*   London; New York:Routledge, 2008.

Warren, Bernie. *Disability and Social Performance.* Cambridge, MA: Brookline Books Inc.,   1988.

Warren, Bernie. *Drama Games.* Concord, ON: Captus Press, 1996.

Way, Brian. *Development Through Drama.* London: Longman Group Ltd., 1967.

Wolfensberger, Wolf. *A Brief Introduction to Social Role Valorisation: A High-Order Concept for Addressing the Plight of Societally Devalued People, and for Structuring Human Services.* 3rd ed. Syracuse, NY: Training Institute for Human Service Planning, Leadership and Change Agency, Syracuse University, 1998.

Related Websites

- Center for Plain Language, "Plain Language"
  <http://www.centerforplainlanguage.org/>

- Fanelli, Leslie. "Disability Pride"—Theatre in Motion's musical soundtrack to their songful play, *Disability Pride*, featuring original anthems of the Disability Rights Movement
  <http://www.cdbaby.com/cd/theatreinmotion2>

- Kerr, Laura. "Laura Kerr, PhD, IMFT | Trauma's Labyrinth"
  <http://www.laurakkerr.com/about/>

- "National Arts Disability Centre"
  <http://www.nadc.ucla.edu>

- Plain Language Action and Information Network (PLAIN) "PlainLanguage.gov: Improving Communication"
  <http://www.plainlanguage.gov/site/about.cfm>

- Play With Perspective Ltd.
  < http://www.playwithperspective.com>

- University of California Berkeley 2010 "Disability Rights and Independent Living Movements"
  <http://bancroft.berkeley.edu/collections/drilm/index.html >

- "VSA"
  <http://www.kennedy-

center.org/education/vsa>

- Wolbring, Gregor. "Ableism and Ability
  Ethics and Governance Blog"
  <http://ableism.wordpress.com>

- Wolbring, Gregor, et al. "What Sorts of
  People"
  <http://whatsortsofpeople.wordpress.com/>

- Wolbring, Gregor. "International Center for
  Bioethics, Culture and Disability"
  <http://www.bioethicsanddisability.org/>

- Wolbring, Gregor. "Nano and Nano- Bio, Info,
  Cogno, Neuro, Synbio, Geo, Chem…"
  <http://wolbring.wordpress.com/>

- "World Institute on Disability"
  <http://www.wid.org/>

Appendix 1: Nineteen Underlying Principles

The following is a list of expanded, underlying principles used by InsideOut. Note that a lesser number of these principles originated from an undergraduate course, "Using the Creative Arts in Rehabilitation," taught by Dr. Bernie Warren at the University of Calgary. The list was expanded as I put the theory into practice with InsideOut. Thereafter, I taught the aforementioned course, and made it my own.

1.   The Artist versus the artist: From a theatrical perspective, each of us has the right to be creative, to be artists. The Artists are the well-known professionals.

2.   The creative arts are emotional in nature and promote healthy emotional expression.

3.   The use of the creative arts in virtually any setting is limited only by our willingness and creativity.

4.   The creative arts can be adapted to almost any group or population and, as a facilitator, you are responsible for meeting the needs of your group or population.

5.   Physical and emotional safety is paramount.

6.   There are no wrong answers.

7.   The creative arts are 'a-scriptive' rather than 'pre-scriptive'. An 'a-scriptive' model focuses on ascribing the strengths of the individual to the process. A 'pre-scriptive' model tends to focus on deficits.

8.   The creative arts mediate between (or bridge) inner and outer reality.

9.   All individuals have the right to creative expression.

10.   All the arts – drama, music, dance, storytelling, painting, and drawing – are healing and aid in the integration of mind, body, and spirit.

11.   The creative arts empower all individuals through their ability to express our unique   creative thumbprint, and are especially useful with preverbal and nonverbal populations.

12.   The five symbol systems through which we learn are numbers, words, images, gestures, and sound.

13.   The creative arts integrate left- and right-brain functions.

14.   The creative arts are consistent with the concept of multiple intelligences (e.g., the   works of Howard Gardner, Leslie Fanelli, and others).

15.   The creative arts are the expression of the soul.

16.   At the therapeutic end, participants and clients leave with "generalisable" skills.

17.   The creative arts should promote laughter and be enjoyable.

18.   The nature of activities is cooperative rather than competitive, and they foster group cohesiveness.

19.   The creative arts promote personal confidence and develop interpersonal skills.

Appendix 2: Ground Rules (example)

This is a sample, as each group develops its own set of ground rules at the beginning of each season/session. Rules may be added or subtracted throughout a season/session.

1.   Arrive on time.

2.   If you are unable to arrive on time, please call to notify the group.

3.   Wear loose, comfortable clothing; no dangling earrings, etc.

4.   Treat one another with respect at all times; listening is very important.

5.   Excessive profanity is discouraged, unless it is a part of a production; speak kindly to one another.

6.   No chewing gum.

7.   No cell phones on.

8.   Each actor has the right to perform; there are no one-actor shows.